ALSO BY MICHAEL TOUGIAS

Fatal Forecast:
An Incredible True Tale of Disaster and Survival at Sea

Ten Hours Until Dawn:
The True Story of Heroism and Tragedy Aboard the Can Do

The Finest Hours:
The True Story of the U.S. Coast Guard's Most Daring Sea Rescue
(coauthor: Casey Sherman)

Until I Have No Country:
A Novel of King Philip's Indian War

King Philip's War:
The History and Legacy of America's Forgotten Conflict
(coauthor: Eric Schultz)

Quabbin:
A History and Explorers Guide

The Blizzard of '78

River Days:
Exploring the Connecticut River from Source to Sea

Exploring the Hidden Charles

There's a Porcupine in My Outhouse:
Misadventures of a Mountain Man Wannabe

OVERBOARD!

A TRUE BLUE-WATER ODYSSEY OF DISASTER AND SURVIVAL

MICHAEL J. TOUGIAS

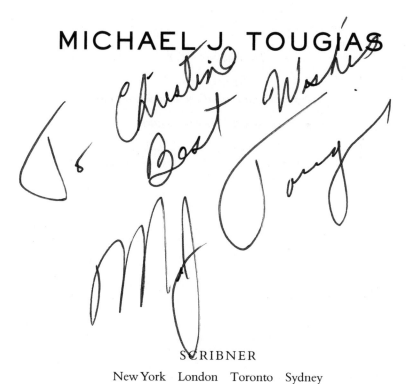

SCRIBNER

New York   London   Toronto   Sydney

SCRIBNER

A Division of Simon & Schuster, Inc.
1230 Avenue of the Americas
New York, NY 10020

Copyright © 2010 by Michael Tougias

All rights reserved, including the right to reproduce this book or portions thereof
in any form whatsoever. For information address Scribner Subsidiary Rights Department,
1230 Avenue of the Americas, New York, NY 10020.

First Scribner hardcover edition March 2010

SCRIBNER and design are registered trademarks of The Gale Group, Inc.,
used under license by Simon & Schuster, Inc., the publisher of this work.

For information about special discounts for bulk purchases,
please contact Simon & Schuster Special Sales at 1-866-506-1949
or business@simonandschuster.com.

The Simon & Schuster Speakers Bureau can bring authors to your live event.
For more information or to book an event, contact the Simon & Schuster Speakers Bureau
at 1-866-248-3049 or visit our website at www.simonspeakers.com.

Manufactured in the United States of America

2   4   6   8   10   9   7   5   3   1

Library of Congress Cataloging-in-Publication Data is available.

ISBN   978-1-4391-4574-6
ISBN   978-1-4391-5362-8 (ebook)

PHOTOGRAPH CREDITS:
Images 1, 2, 3, 11, and 12 appear courtesy of the Tighe family.
Images 4 and 15 appear courtesy of the Reidy family.
Images 5, 9, and 10 appear courtesy of the Burd family.
Image 6 appears courtesy of the Gilchrist family.
Image 7 appears courtesy of the Ferrer family.
Image 8 appears courtesy of the National Weather Service.
Image 13 appears courtesy of the U.S. Coast Guard.
Image 14 appears courtesy of the U.S. Navy.

*To the people caught in the storm
and those who tried to rescue them*

CONTENTS

CONTENTS

PART THREE

PROLOGUE

The Gulf Stream is a moving mass of seawater that flows in a north-northeast trajectory off the eastern coast of the United States. Its warm waters are a result of its origination in the Gulf of Mexico, where the equatorial currents swirl clockwise within the Gulf of Mexico and then shoot northeast through the gap between Cuba and Florida. From here, this river of salt water, approximately a quarter of a mile deep, flows northward along the coast of Florida at approximately five knots. It continues northward along the outer limits of the U.S. continental shelf until it reaches Cape Hatteras, North Carolina, where the Gulf Stream broadens and runs in a more northeasterly progression at a diminishing speed of two to three knots. Along its route this moving mass of water spins out enormous warm-water eddies that vary in size and location. Incredibly, the Gulf Stream crosses the entire North Atlantic all the way to the British Isles, where its warmth is still strong enough to moderate the European climate—which is why there are palm trees in southern England.

The volume of water in the Gulf Stream is so immense that it has been estimated the flow carries twenty-five times more water than all the rivers in the world combined. Because of this enormous quantity of water the Gulf Stream remains a separate entity and mixes only slightly with the surrounding ocean. On its eastern side is an area of the Atlantic called the Sargasso Sea, where the water temperature is typically in the 70s. Beyond the west-northwest side of the Gulf Stream (often referred to as the North Wall), however, the waters of the continental shelf are much colder, and in May are in the upper 50s. Sailors coming from the west can literally see the temperature rise quite dramatically as they enter the Gulf Stream, watching it climb to 70 degrees in the outer fringes and then into the low 80s toward the center of the current. During calm conditions sailors can actually detect a change in the hue of the ocean from dark blue off the continental shelf to cobalt blue in the Gulf Stream and Sargasso Sea, and the effect can be quite beautiful. In stormy conditions, however, the Gulf Stream can strike terror in a sailor, as the effect of the wind against its current produces enormous waves, often steep and breaking. And sometimes, from out of the blue, a monster wave—a rogue wave—is formed, which can spell disaster.

In early May of 2005 two sailboats, the *Almeisan* and the *At Ease,* were in the Gulf Stream when they were overtaken by a horrific storm. The crews can blame the Gulf Stream for the size of the waves that put them in peril, yet one sailor can credit this moving river of seawater for helping to keep him alive in the terrible hours he struggled within the storm-tossed seas. His incredible survival borders on the miraculous.

PART I

CHAPTER ONE

PREPARATIONS AND A NEW CREW

Tuesday, May 3, 2005

As Chris Ferrer steps aboard the *Almeisan,* a smile spreads across his face as he thinks how the days of planning and buying gear are behind him, replaced by the trip itself. The Hardin forty-five-foot sailboat will soon carry him on his first lengthy offshore voyage— more than 600 miles of blue-water sailing from Black Rock Harbor in Bridgeport, Connecticut, to Bermuda. The boat doesn't rock as Chris puts his full weight on the deck, and he likes its solid feel, a full seventeen feet longer than his own sailboat. He can't wait to get under way.

Muffled noises rise from below, and Chris steps down the companionway ladder, shouting a hello before he reaches the bottom. Captain Tom Tighe and first mate Lochlin Reidy look up from their chores and walk toward Chris, offering their hands and welcoming him to what will be his temporary, floating home for the next several days. Chris returns the greetings, but his eyes scan the space around him, and he doesn't like what he sees. Gear and supplies lie scattered about, and it's clear there are several hours of work to do before the crew embarks. He shakes off his disappointment and asks what he can do to help.

Chris learned of the opportunity to go on this voyage through a service, Offshore Passage Opportunities, which matches interested crew with captains, their boats, and the destination. A crossing to Bermuda was something the thirty-four-year-old molecular biologist and information technology administrator had been wanting to do for a long time, both for the adventure of the trip and the offshore

3

experience to be gained by being an active crewmember rather than just a passenger. He thought that someday he might buy a bigger boat, and he wanted to learn all that he could about blue-water sailing. That was the very reason he chose the *Almeisan* and Captain Tighe, a skipper who enjoyed sharing his knowledge gained from forty-eight crossings between the United States and Bermuda.

Chris is five feet eight inches tall, of average build, with short brown hair, brown eyes, and glasses. He's got a quick, ready smile, a strong voice, and a sharp mind, which he puts to good use with an irreverent sense of humor. He's the type of person who can walk into a party, not know a soul, and within minutes be engaged in comfortable conversation, making people around him laugh. Married, Chris will soon become a father—one more reason to make this voyage now, before parenting duties demand more of his free time.

In preparation for the trip, Chris has followed Captain Tighe's instructions to purchase a yellow foul-weather suit, safety harness, boots, and leather-palmed gloves, as well as an airline ticket for the return trip from Bermuda. This will be a one-way trip for Chris, and Tighe will make the return voyage with a new crew who will be waiting in Bermuda. In addition to the mandatory personal gear, Tom has asked him to read the 300-page *Almeisan* cruise manual, an incredibly detailed body of work produced by the captain that covers everything from duties to be performed while on watch to the operation of safety equipment.

One of the first things Chris learned from the manual was that the name *Almeisan* (pronounced Al-may-sin) is the name of a bright star, and in Arabic means "proudly marching one." Chris appreciates the work that went into the manual and considers it a positive reflection of the captain, who wishes to have his crew know the vessel inside and out. Tom has seemingly thought of everything entailed in sailing to Bermuda, including a section on passage dynamics that begins by stating:

> An ocean passage on a small yacht will be a new experience for many. You should be prepared to experience mood swings. As we leave, you may wonder why you are doing this. Remember when you decided to make the passage for your answer. You will surely wonder why you

made the trip when we encounter heavy weather. When the weather is good you will be glad you made the trip and think it is a great experience. Your recollection of the trip later will most likely only include the good times.

Chris is not planning on any mood swings, because even during difficult times in his life he rarely sinks too low, having figured out—even at his relatively young age—that while he may not be able to control events, he can control his reactions. Staying upbeat has become almost second nature.

As Chris works on the deck, fastening halyards and jacklines, he gets his first good look at the *Almeisan*. The yacht has a ketch rig; two masts with the taller mast forward and the shorter mast aft. The headsails and mainsail are equipped with manual furling mechanisms, which can be set and trimmed from the cockpit. A cruising spinnaker and a mizzen staysail increase the boat's sailing capability. The height above the waterline to the top of the mainmast is fifty-three feet. Chris knows the boat—built in 1981—is not new, but the equipment appears to be in fine shape. The *Almeisan*'s cockpit with hardtop dodger is just aft of center, and can be completely enclosed with canvas curtains and plastic windows. On deck, directly forward of the cockpit, are two translucent Plexiglas hatches measuring two feet by five feet. These provide illumination for the salon below. The fiberglass boat's large foredeck has a teak overlay; it's a great place to soak up the sun on calm and clear days.

Looking up from his inspection of the boat, Chris sees a woman carrying a duffel bag walking down the dock toward him. He knows this must be Kathy Gilchrist, the second paying crewmember. When she arrives at the *Almeisan,* Chris greets her and welcomes her aboard.

Like Chris, Kathy is making the trip to learn more about offshore sailing and for the new experience of going on a long voyage. But unlike Chris, she's having second thoughts.

Kathy, age forty-six and single, is a legal secretary from New Jersey who learned about boating aboard her father's powerboat. After her father passed away, she missed being on the water and decided to try sailing, joined a club, and sailed with friends as often as possible.

She later took several navigation courses and crewed on overnight sailing trips. As the years went by the allure of a longer voyage under sail, particularly one to Bermuda, prompted her to start reading more on offshore sailing. She met Captain Tighe while shopping for a book on the Gulf Stream at a large retail store, Landfall Navigation, where Tom worked part-time. Tom, sixty-five years old, had retired from his career in industrial sales, but he wasn't ready to slow down. He pursued his passion of sailing by putting in a few hours each week at Landfall Navigation, performing custom boat work, and teaching his Bermuda Bound Blue-Water Sailing Seminar. However, the days he most looked forward to were those on the water, sailing with his wife, children, grandchildren, and friends.

When Kathy met Tom at the store, she happened to mention her interest in sailing someday to Bermuda, and Tom explained a bit about the trips he made. He gave her his card and suggested she check out his website to learn more, which she did. A few months later Tom emailed her and suggested she take his course and possibly go on an upcoming Bermuda voyage set for May. Before she committed to join his crew, Kathy first took Tom's blue-water sailing course, which she enjoyed. She told Tom she wanted to go on the Bermuda trip, but explained she thought May might be a little early for her first offshore trip. Tom assured her that May was a good time for the trip, and said that whenever she had watch duty he would be scheduled to share it with her. Reassured, she signed on for the voyage.

But now, standing on the boat for the first time, Kathy wonders again if she has made the right decision. Although it's a beautiful spring day, the timing of the trip still seems too early in the season, and she thinks there will likely be some cold days and unpredictable weather out at sea. But that's not what's really bothering her, and she can't articulate the feeling. For a moment she thinks about how to tell Tom she has decided not to go. But then her strong sense of loyalty, commitment, and responsibility assert themselves, and she tries to shoo away the nagging feeling of uncertainty. *Well,* she says to herself, *it's too late to back out now. They're counting on me.*

Tom and Loch come up from below and chat with Kathy and Chris for a few moments. The captain explains that the fifth and final crewmember will be arriving soon, and he shows the two new crewmembers more tasks that need to be done on deck, and Kathy and Chris get busy. It's midafternoon, and the scheduled departure time is set for midnight to take advantage of the outgoing tides. Tom shows Kathy the yellow emergency "ditch" canisters stored in a box on the aft deck, and asks her to divide a carton of protein bars into each container. Chris jokes to Kathy that she should slip in a few extra bars in his bag because he gets cranky when he's hungry. The two new crewmembers then rig the running backstays, and attend to other minor tasks.

Chris and Kathy later pause in their work and go below to ask Tom a question about the equipment. Tom and Loch are giving the four-cylinder, sixty-five horsepower engine a final check. Earlier they had filled the boat's two fuel tanks with 180 gallons of diesel— enough fuel to power the vessel the entire trip to Bermuda should there be no wind, an unlikely scenario. Kathy notices the supplies and equipment scattered about, and has the feeling Tom is in a rush as he walks with her and Chris back up on deck. Never having been on a lengthy offshore trip, Kathy tells herself that the many last-minute chores and stowing of gear is normal, but she worries Tom won't have time to review the boat's equipment with her prior to departure. She wants to understand how everything functions in as much detail as possible before the *Almeisan* is under way.

The third guest crewmember, Ron Burd, arrives at the boat and is able to dive right into the work because he owns a sailboat and has made many trips up and down the East Coast, from his home in New Hampshire to Florida. He's never sailed to Bermuda, how-ever, and wants to gain a little firsthand experience before he makes the voyage with his own boat. Ron, an engineer, is the oldest of the group at age seventy, but he's in better shape than most men twenty years younger. He has short gray hair, a neatly trimmed gray beard, and is not prone to idle chatter, yet in his own reserved way is quite friendly.

At around 6 p.m. Tom calls the crew and they gather below. He explains that he and Loch were cleaning up and that they not only had to stow away all the food and supplies for the trip to Bermuda, but that they had to do the same for the return trip. He shows the crew to their quarters so they can unpack their gear. The interior of the *Almeisan* is crafted of teak and mahogany, with two double berths and four single berths, each with an oscillating fan and reading light. The salon has an L-shaped seating arrangement around a dining table, as well as a fold-down chart table that can double as a serving platform. A galley with a double sink and two nearby heads (bathrooms) with hot water and shower round out the crew's quarters.

When the crew has stowed their personal gear they take a break for sandwiches and talk about the trip and their backgrounds. These five people—most of them total strangers to one another—slowly get to know each other. For the next five or six days they will be confined to a small space on a seemingly endless ocean. Getting along is crucial on such a trip, but never guaranteed. After three or four days a person's idiosyncrasies can wear on the nerves of shipmates. Crews can become surly, sullen, and irritable, making the captain's job a nightmare. On the other hand, discovering another person's sense of humor, knowledge, and life stories can form bonds that lead to lifelong friendships.

The crew does not expect to receive radio messages or calls from loved ones once they are under way, and Captain Tighe's manual makes this clear: "Do not ask anyone to call us in an emergency because they most likely will not be able to contact us. There is nothing we will be able to do to help them, and their problem will only cause you distress on your vacation." It's good advice, and Tom wants his crew to understand the voyage is quite different from a day sail. Nevertheless, Tom does have a coordinator and general helper on land, logistician Donna Christman, and he will check in with her by radio every other day. If an emergency arises on land, she will confer with Tom before he decides how to tell the affected crewmember.

Of course the crew will be busy for much of the trip, performing duties from cooking to handling the sails, and a good chunk of the time will be spent standing four-hour watches. To the nonsailor the watch responsibilities may seem excessively regimented, but the overriding reason for a watch is safety, and Captain Tighe emphasizes the point. He requires the crewmember scheduled for watch to report fifteen minutes early; wear the orange watch hat, shoes, and safety harness; and carry a knife and whistle. Tom will post duties for each assigned period, but on all shifts the person standing watch must keep the yacht on course, be on the lookout for other ships and floating debris, and plot the yacht's present position in case the electronic navigation equipment fails. On all night watches or in heavy weather, two people will be on watch together.

After the sandwiches are consumed, Kathy is glad that the captain takes the newcomers on a walk-through of the boat, explaining how each piece of equipment is operated. Her focus intensifies when Tom discusses emergency equipment and procedures, in part because she lost a close friend at sea. Sailing alone, her friend was delivering a boat in the Caribbean, and he was on a tight schedule. The National Weather Service had been tracking a hurricane hundreds of miles away, and there was a chance it could swing toward the region her friend was sailing in. Rather than head toward the nearest port, the skipper weighed the odds, and decided to continue toward his originally planned destination. The decision cost him his life when his boat capsized in the hurricane.

Tom first shows the crew where the fire extinguishers, flashlights, life jackets, life rings, life sling, and medical kit are located. Then he gives a basic overview of the engine, the fuel and propane shut-off valves, battery disconnect switches, and radios. The boat is equipped with an Emergency Position Indicating Radio Beacon (EPIRB), and Tom explains that once it is activated a signal is sent to a satellite, which relays the location of the emergency to the Coast Guard. Next, Tom points out the location of the rented life raft, which has a dome-shaped canopy and ballast bags beneath for added stability. Quoting from an old adage, Tom says, "If you get off the yacht to abandon ship, step up to the life raft." In other words, explains Tom, we only abandon the boat if it is actually sinking.

It is now 10 p.m., and there are still a couple of hours before the high tide they want for a favorable departure through Long Island Sound. Ron Burd is interested in the engine, so he and Tom head back to the engine compartment and discuss the pros and cons of the various motors they have used over the years. The others put on sweatshirts and head topside to take another look at the cockpit. The wooden steering wheel, mounted waist high, dominates the center of the cockpit, and a binnacle, the case that contains the navigational instruments, is mounted forward of that. Above the binnacle, facing the helmsman is the electronic navigation display, autopilot remote, and sensors for wind, depth, and speed. Mounted on the hardtop ceiling above the cockpit are the VHF transceiver, intercom, and small electronic chart, which hangs from the ceiling on brackets.

The group talks for a while longer, and it seems to Chris they've been at the dock for a week. At 11:30 Tom announces it is close enough to midnight to get under way. This gives a jolt of energy to the crew, who have grown weary from the long day.

As they leave Black Rock Harbor and begin heading east toward Montauk to round the eastern tip of Long Island, the weather is so gentle there's not even a breath of a breeze. The ocean is unruffled and welcoming, and the stars above—one of them with the same name as the boat—glitter more brightly as the *Almeisan* motors away from the artificial lights of civilization. Now everyone is too excited to think about sleep.

CHAPTER TWO

TOM AND LOCH

Before the *Almeisan* left Black Rock Harbor, Captain Tighe made frequent climbs up the companionway to check on the progress his new crew was making topside. He had always felt the best way to really know a boat was through a hands-on approach, and it was also the quickest way to make the crew feel part of the team. This also gave the captain a chance to gauge each person's true sailing experience before they hit open water. He made safety his number one priority, and if a crewmember needed a little extra help performing his duties, Tom was more than happy to oblige.

Usually, there were very few surprises from the crew because Tom conducted an interview with each and every person who showed an interest in making the voyage to Bermuda. He wanted sailors to know that there might be hardships during the sail, and that it was not going to be a week of pure relaxation. Sometimes, all it took were a few minutes of conversation for Tom to realize that the prospective crewmember just wasn't going to be the right fit, and he would diplomatically tell them as much. Other times it would take a few conversations to realize that the person's expectations and the reality of the voyage differed. Having the crew read his manual was another way to see if they were serious about the educational aspect of the trip or if they were naively thinking that sailing six hundred miles in a forty-five-foot boat was a piece of cake. Tom certainly didn't want a high-strung individual to come unglued if they sailed into nasty weather. In some instances, he sensed a cockiness in a sailor who seemed to give the manual and safety procedures lip service only, and Tom would weed that person out before any agreement was made. This process of getting to know a potential crewmember prior to a trip was so important that Tom insisted on conducting the interviews in person rather than over the phone or by email. By meeting face-to-face, Tom often found the answer to one of his litmus-test questions: Is this person someone I'd want to spend several days in a life raft with? If the answer was no, he looked for a different crewmember.

His reputation in local sailing circles was one of complete competence, and many sailors consulted him about everything from equipment to the weather. Tom took seamanship seriously. But he also knew the therapeutic power of sailing, and this was an important aspect he hoped crewmembers would discover while blue-water sailing—something totally different from the grind of their daily lives. In fact, he often tried to time the *Almeisan*'s arrival at the Gulf Stream for evening, so that passengers could see and sense the wonder of this moving mass of ocean.

The Gulf Stream, with its warm water, often creates its own mini weather system, especially along its western edge, where it slides by the colder surrounding water off the continental shelf. Sometimes, particularly at dusk, heat lightning dances across the water or shoots from cloud to cloud. During the daytime, Tom would encourage his crew to just lie back on the deck and watch the strange cloud formations that constantly reshaped themselves over the Gulf Stream. He wanted his crew to have a total experience while on the *Almeisan*—education, adventure, camaraderie, and appreciation for nature.

Tom used the trips as a way to share his knowledge, and he only asked that the crew contribute to the cost of fuel, food, and the rented life raft. He simply loved introducing a novice sailor to the new world of an offshore voyage, and his outgoing personality and sense of humor made him a natural teacher. Many of his passengers left his vessel not only with more confidence in their seamanship, but also knowing more about themselves. Often they made permanent friendships with crewmembers, and a few returned to the *Almeisan* for several more trips to Bermuda.

And that was how green-eyed Lochlin Reidy, age fifty-eight, became Tom's first mate on this voyage. Loch first met Tom in the late 1970s, after a friend of Loch's had described a fantastic sailing trip he took to Bermuda on a sailboat named the *Almeisan*. The more

Loch listened, the more the story reminded him of his carefree days as a boy on Long Island, near Little Neck Bay. When he was just sixteen years old, Loch and his friends built a twenty-four-foot sailboat that they sailed and occasionally raced on Long Island Sound. Then came college, followed by a two-year stint in the army, and the course of his life took him away from sailing. He was married at twenty-one, and soon became the father of two boys, Peter and Steven, supporting his family as a technician for Southern New England Telephone.

Loch was thirty-two years old when he decided he had been away from the ocean too long. His marriage had ended in divorce, and he decided a long blue-water sailing trip would be the perfect pick-me-up. Loch asked his friend for Tom Tighe's telephone number and called him up, and Tom had him put his name on the list for the next trip.

Prior to the voyage Tom interviewed Loch, and the two men hit it off. On Loch's first excursion on the *Almeisan* he felt like a teenager again, and was surprised how well the crew of five strangers meshed. Then he realized their amiability was not an accident but rather the result of Tom's careful screening. The crew had a real mix of experience, from complete sailing novices to sailors who owned their own boats, but everyone pitched in with the work, and the five-day sail to Bermuda was a joy. Once in Bermuda, Tom stayed on the boat and got her, and a new crew, ready for the return trip, while Loch and the rest of the outgoing crew left the *Almeisan* and enjoyed the island, staying at hotels before catching a flight home.

The trip was such a nice change of pace for Loch that the next year he did it again. Although Tom lived in New York and Loch in Connecticut, they got together occasionally in the off-season to talk about sailing and their plans for the summer. Before long, Loch was helping Tom at his Bermuda Bound sailing seminars, and was on the Bermuda voyage nearly every year. Loch began to know the workings of the *Almeisan* almost as well as Tom, and it was natural that on the trips he made, he would be the first mate, helping to train new crews and answer their many questions. He was soft-spoken and unassuming, and novice sailors valued his patience. The May 2005 trip would be Loch's sixteenth voyage with Tom, and every year he seemed to appreciate those days at sea with an increasing sense of gratitude. In the few years that he did not make the trip, Loch felt his summer was incomplete.

Both Tom and Loch had easygoing personalities; quick minds that could solve almost any problem, including technical ones; and, of course, a love of the sea. From a distance the men might even pass as brothers—both had gray-brown hair and were about five foot nine and heavy-set. Tom, however, wore glasses and at sixty-five was seven years older than Loch. Although quite active for his age, he did confide to Loch that he wanted to slow down a bit and that this would be his last voyage to Bermuda. The return trip would mark his fiftieth passage, and he thought that would be a nice round number to finish on.

Loch was now remarried. His two sons were grown and on their own, and Loch and his second wife, Sandra, were raising their own daughter, Ashley, who was thirteen. Sandra also had a daughter, Denise, from an earlier marriage, and Denise enjoyed Loch's company so much she accompanied Loch on two *Almeisan* voyages to Bermuda in her earlier twenties. Ashley had been day sailing on the *Almeisan* and like her stepsister wanted to make the trip to Bermuda with her father. Loch, however, felt she was a bit young for the passage, and told her she would get her chance soon enough.

Now, with the hectic pace of the final day's preparations behind him, and the boat under way, Loch relaxes in the cockpit of the *Almeisan,* chatting with Ron, Kathy, and Chris. He tells himself, *Tom's done it again, he's put together just the right crew.*

Loch thinks that the only thing that would make these first hours of the voyage even better would be the sound of sails fluttering rather than the drone of the diesel engine. But the stars are out, the company is good, and Loch thinks about the fun days ahead. He wonders if Tom really will "retire" from making these Bermuda trips, knowing that if he does, this may be his own farewell voyage as well.

As the excitement of getting under way subsides, crewmembers not on watch drift below for sleep. The *Almeisan* is motoring almost due east, directly across the placid waters of Long Island Sound. In five days, if all goes well, they will dock in St. George's, Bermuda.

CHAPTER THREE

A WARNING

Sunshine streams down on the *Almeisan* on Wednesday morning as the boat turns south, passing through Plum Gut off Long Island's Orient Point. By noon the *Almeisan* rounds the tip of Long Island at Montauk and is in the open waters of the North Atlantic, heading in a southeasterly direction. The gray seas are relatively calm, with wave heights of one to two feet, and the air is still, dashing the crew's hopes that they would be able to raise some sails once outside of Long Island Sound.

Ron Burd especially wants wind, and he even hopes for a bit of heavy weather, wishing to learn all he can from Tom—in all kinds of conditions—before he attempts to make a similar offshore voyage on his own boat. The former U.S. Marine and businessman has recently retired, selling his civil engineering company in New Hampshire, and he finally has more time to spend on the water.

Ron perks up when he hears Tom on the radio, talking to a ketch traveling north. Tom learns that the ketch is heading to Nova Scotia, and he jokes to the passing captain that they are going the wrong way, meaning that the warm weather is behind them. The captain on the other boat, however, is dead serious when he responds, "No, *you're* going the wrong way. There's a low-pressure system forming off the Carolinas."

Tom already knows about this forecast and answers, "Well, we'll take the good with the bad."

Tom and Loch know the low-pressure system is expected to move due north, just off the coastline. They estimate that by the time the low is as far north as the *Almeisan*'s position, they will be well to the east of the system's center, and out of danger.

The crew has listened to the exchange between the captains on the radio, and Tom assures them that if a gale does take shape, the *Almeisan* will be a safe distance away. He explains that during many of his Bermuda trips he encounters heavy weather, and the *Almeisan* is more than capable of getting through it. He does not volunteer specifics about the weather forecasts he's heard, and Ron and Chris don't dwell on the ominous words of the captain from the other sailboat. Kathy, however, finds it difficult to do the same. Her thoughts go back to her friend who drowned when he tried to stay on schedule while sailing. *We're just off Montauk,* she tells herself, *we can go into port at New York City.* Kathy knows she's the only one thinking this, but still considers asking Tom to drop her off in New York. Then her sense of responsibility and obligation pushes the thought away.

That evening Tom serves a lobster stew his wife made just prior to the trip. The seas are still tranquil, almost glassy, and the air temperature is a comfortable 65 degrees. Loch is talking about the approaching sunset and explains how he once saw the unusual green flash that sometimes occurs at the moment the sun dips below the watery horizon. "And when we get to the Gulf Stream, it has its own microclimate. Not only is the water warmer, but the air also. Each crossing is different, but all of them—at least for me—are extraordinary experiences." He explains that one of the main reasons he takes this yearly trip is that nothing else can rival the feeling of being so close to nature.

On Thursday morning there's a hint of wind, and the crew is upbeat as they watch dolphins race in the bow wave of the boat and whales breach off the port side, making Loch's comments about nature seem prescient. Under motor, the *Almeisan* makes about six knots, continuing on its southeast course. By late morning, a bit of breeze blows, and the crew is finally able to set the mainsail. A three- to four-foot swell rolls beneath the boat, rocking it gently from side to side. Tom explains that they will soon be crossing the continental shelf, and he keeps the motor running, knowing they are a bit behind schedule.

Everyone is enjoying himself, but Kathy continues to be concerned about the low-pressure system coming up the coast. She keeps the worry to herself, not wanting to put a damper on the good mood and great chemistry of the crew. Still, she can't help but pay close attention to the marine weather reports occasionally announced on the radio. And even though she does not fully understand what is being said with regard to the various geographic positions given on the broadcast, she hears enough to know that the ride is going to be a lot rougher in the coming days.

Tom, sensing her apprehension, tells her not to lose any sleep over it, and to let him worry about the weather. Ever prudent, though, Tom has the crew make preparations for heavy weather. The anchor rode (rope) is disconnected from the Danforth anchor so that the rode can be stowed belowdecks, and the anchor is secured to the bow pulpit. Spinnaker halyards are secured to the bulwark, and hatches are dogged down. When the work is done, Kathy, Ron, and Chris pass a couple of hours playing cards, while Tom and Loch stand watch.

Tom makes beef stew for dinner, and everyone except Chris enjoys the meal. Chris is feeling queasy—the first inkling of sea-sickness is upon him—as the swells grow to five feet. He tries to stay active, plotting the Gulf Stream on the chart and stowing the trash on the aft deck in an orange nylon bag tied to the rail. But by 8 p.m.—about the time it begins raining—Chris is vomiting. He is not prone to seasickness, but is so ill he is unable to stand watch. Going below deck only makes his nausea worse, so he remains in the cockpit, spending much of the time lying on the deck.

Kathy feels fine physically, but seeing Chris become seasick, coupled with the rising seas, brings back her sense of unease. She asks Tom about the latest weather forecast, and he again says it's nothing to worry about, reminding her that they are approaching the Gulf Stream, where it typically gets a little rough. She isn't buying the explanation, but instead thinks they are feeling the leading edge of the storm.

Approximately 800 miles away, off the Georgia coast, the low-pressure system is disorganized, and cloud cover extends far out to sea. Earlier that day, the ill-defined system crossed over Florida, heading in a northeasterly direction, picking up moisture from the ocean. Reports show that pressure gradients, which funnel the wind in a counterclockwise direction—characteristic of all lows—are not tightly packed, and wind gusts barely exceed twenty-five knots. Satellite images do not yet reveal an "eye" or clear center to the system, but instead show a broken yet massive ceiling of cloud cover, extending south off the Florida coast and north all the way to Virginia. At this time the system is slow-moving, and meteorologists aren't certain what will come of it, but one thing is clear: it's heading north, directly toward the *Almeisan.*

Estimated Position of *The Almeisan*

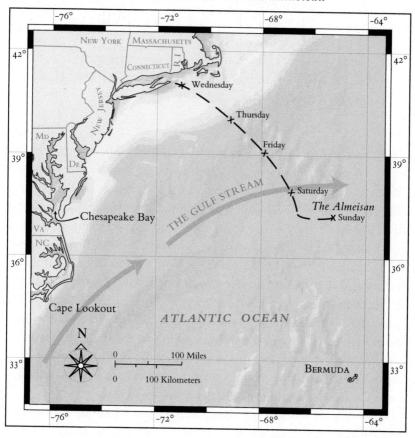

CHAPTER FOUR

THE STORM'S FIRST JAB

For Chris Ferrer, Thursday night seems like an eternity. He is either vomiting out one of the windows in the canvas curtain of the *Almeisan*'s cockpit or curled up in the fetal position on the cockpit sole (deck). Chris feels guilty about not taking his watch or doing his share of chores, but the seasickness is totally debilitating, and the ocean is not helping him, with five- and six-foot swells now rolling the boat up and down, side to side. His crewmates offer comforting words, and remind him to take sips of water, knowing he could easily become dehydrated. Chris follows their advice, but figures he's vomiting out fluids faster than his body can absorb them. He's completely fatigued, so much so that crawling to the window becomes a major undertaking. He just wants to make it through the night, thinking that perhaps in the morning he will have become acclimated to the boat's motion, and the nausea will pass.

Chris's body is receiving conflicting signals regarding movement and balance, which results in seasickness. While the vestibular system of his inner ear is transmitting to his brain the motion of the waves, his eyes are equalizing the movement, telling the brain that he's relatively stable because he is moving with the boat. The brain, trying to decipher the conflicting signals, becomes confused, triggering dizziness, nausea, and exhaustion. Some theories even suggest that the brain concludes that the disoriented feeling is the result of poisoning, which triggers vomiting to rid the body of toxins.

To Chris, the vomiting feels like the worst part of seasickness, but dehydration is the issue to really worry about. Sailors can lose so much bodily fluid from vomiting that they can go into shock. Symptoms include shallow breathing, confusion, lightheadedness, a weak but fast pulse, and even loss of consciousness. Shock, never the kind of thing you want to suffer, is especially dangerous far out at sea.

Tolerance for motion can vary widely from person to person, and the onset of seasickness strikes sailors at different times. The severity of the illness also varies among individuals, and it can be so pronounced some people experience real anxiety that they are so ill they will die. There's an old sailor's saying that seasickness is a fate worse than death: first you're afraid you're going to die—and then you're afraid you won't! Chris hasn't quite reached that point, but he is questioning the wisdom of making this passage to Bermuda.

Earlier in the day, when Chris first felt ill, he went out on the deck and tried looking out at the horizon, so that his visual clues— watching the horizon rise and fall with the seas—would match the motion his inner ear was sensing. It was the right technique, but unfortunately for Chris it didn't work; the *Almeisan*'s pitching and rolling were just too disorienting for his central nervous system. Now, in the darkness, with the hour approaching midnight, Chris is just trying to let time pass, knowing that eventually—usually within twenty-four to forty-eight hours after the onset of seasickness—his body should adapt to the conditions around him.

A leaden sky emerges slowly from the blackness of night, and Friday morning is the first day of the voyage with sustained wind. Seas have now grown to seven feet and the wind is blowing at about twenty knots. No one has slept particularly well because of the boat's motion. The sense of enjoying the journey and not focusing on the destination is replaced by the single-minded desire to get to Bermuda as quickly as possible. Bermuda, though, is still a long way off: the *Almeisan* is approximately 250 miles east of the coast of Delaware and even farther from Bermuda.

Tom and Loch listen to the latest weather forecast. The wind speeds are expected to be slightly stronger than first thought— perhaps up to thirty-five knots—and the low-pressure system is expected to cover a broader area. There is no doubt that the *Almeisan* crew will be pummeled by the storm for at least the next twenty-four hours. Tom's earlier option of heading back to land is now gone, because the *Almeisan* cannot outrun the storm, and heading west would only put them directly in its path. The captain opts to stay on his present southeast course, hoping that his boat and crew will have escaped the clutches of the gale by Saturday.

Tom hoists a staysail (a triangular headsail) and mizzen (the sail on the rear mast), now that they finally have wind. The wind, however, is strong, too strong, causing the staysail to tear at the head (top), and they have to haul it in. Ron suggests they put out a very small amount of genoa (a large jib that overlaps the mast) but Tom thinks that will only rip as the staysail did. The boat does not have a storm trysail, which is a small sail used in high winds to maintain control and keep the bow to the wind. By late morning, the winds are stronger and somewhat erratic, and Tom decides to take in the one remaining sail, the mizzen, and just slowly motor the boat.

Ron is now beginning to feel queasy, which he finds bewildering because the seventy-year-old has been sailing for more than thirty years and he's never been seasick before. He's been in seas as big as the ones he's currently riding, and he wonders if his nausea has been made worse by something he ate that didn't agree with him. Whatever the cause, by noon he is vomiting and, like Chris, unable to take his turn on watch. Ron lies down on cushioned benches in the galley, and while there he hears Tom on the radio talking to his land-based logistician, Donna Christman. To Ron's ear, Tom sounds cryptic and depressed, and Ron isn't surprised. The sixty-five-year-old captain has had little rest in the last forty-eight hours, and two of his four crewmembers are seasick, with more bad weather on the way. Tom frets about the return trip with a whole new crew, knowing the *Almeisan* is behind schedule, and the seas are slowing the boat's progress to Bermuda.

Adding to the sense of gloom, it begins to shower, and as Friday afternoon progresses, the showers become steady rain, eventually growing into an all-out deluge. Kathy, sitting in the cockpit, watches the rain pound and splatter on the Plexiglas windows, and feels trapped, as if she's going through a never-ending car wash. Luckily, the boat's motion has not affected her, and she and Loch are able to help Tom with the extra workload.

As Friday drags on, the *Almeisan* still performs admirably, rising up and over the dark swells, now ten feet in height. Some waves have become steep, just short of having their crests break. And occasionally, the drumming of the rain is interrupted by the rumble of thunder and flashes of lightning. They are approaching the Gulf Stream, and the lightning does not surprise Loch.

Chris is still seasick, lying in the cockpit, and Loch tries to lighten the mood, telling him, "Well, pretty soon you'll be able to say you crossed the Gulf Stream in a gale."

Loch is doing his best to stay upbeat, but he's not feeling all that great himself. He's not sure if he's just bone weary from too little sleep, or if he too is on the verge of getting seasick. Either way he knows that the constant motion caused by the waves is wearing everyone down. The entire crew is expending energy just by walking, standing or even sitting, as they struggle to keep their balance.

As soon as Loch's watch is over he goes below to try and rest as best he can, hoping to ward off seasickness. It is now Friday evening and Kathy stays on watch with Tom. There is little to say. The *Almeisan* is roughly halfway between the U.S. mainland and Bermuda, utterly alone, and being buffeted about like a cork.

CHAPTER FIVE

THE *AT EASE*

Roughly 300 miles southwest of the *Almeisan*'s position, another sailboat, the *At Ease,* is taking a direct hit from the storm. The two-man crew, captain Bob Cummings and first mate Jerry McCarthy, are even more fatigued than those on the *Almeisan,* and they're kicking themselves for venturing out to sea in the first place. Cummings had been preparing for this voyage for several weeks, and he now knows that he let "the plan" obscure his judgment. He was aware that strong winds and heavy seas could be expected, but the conditions he and McCarthy are now trying to ride out are far worse than were forecast.

Cummings, age forty, is uniquely qualified to make an objective evaluation of his decision making, because he's familiar with high-risk, life-and-death situations from his twenty-year career as a helicopter pilot for the United States Army. He's flown Black Hawks in several of the world's hot spots, seen combat while flying missions during Desert Storm in Iraq, and more recently performed drug interdiction in the Caribbean. Now, caught in the middle of the storm, he's using his military training to keep calm and prioritize his actions. Number one priority: don't do anything to make the situation worse.

Like many sailors, Bob's real passion for the sport began when he bought a small boat, in his case a fourteen-foot Laser, where he learned the fundamentals of sailing and made the most of his time off from flying. The Laser was soon replaced by a twenty-six-foot Tanser sailboat, and a few years later that was sold for a larger vessel, a thirty-nine-foot Oday Aquarius. By this time Bob and his wife had three children, and he was determined to learn all he could about sailing so that trips with his family were not only fun but safe.

He received some of his best training when he first bought the Oday Aquarius. Bob figured he needed a little help on his first extended voyage, and a mutual acquaintance introduced him to longtime sailor and delivery boat captain Jerry McCarthy, who had logged more than 260,000 miles at sea, including eleven transatlantic and two transpacific crossings. The two men hit it off and made an eighteen-hour trip together, followed six months later by a five-day trip.

Jerry, age thirty-five, and Bob have a lot in common besides their passion for sailing. Both men have a great sense of humor, usually dry and understated, and are not afraid of tackling new challenges. They like to keep themselves fit, because their interests involve activities where they're participants rather than spectators. During those initial sailing voyages together they learned that when things don't go as planned, each of them reacts the same way: they roll with the punches, and get to work to resolve the problem.

Jerry was born in Ireland and grew up in London. His love of sailing began when he was seventeen years old. During his senior year in high school, his career counselor suggested he enroll in a sailing program, figuring he would do well in the outdoors since he wasn't wild about sitting in classes all day. And so, upon graduation, Jerry signed on for a one-week training voyage aboard a seventy-two-foot ketch that coasted along the British Isles. He loved the experience. After a few more trips he was invited to be a bosun with the Ocean Youth Club, where he would help train the newcomers, stock the boat with supplies, and organize the trainees into cooking groups.

At age twenty Jerry received his Yacht Master Certificate, and became a yacht delivery captain, delivering boats across the Atlantic. He had a taste of terrible weather right off the bat when he ran into not one but two storms with hurricane-force winds in a single trip. Amazingly, he never got seasick even though he was in bad seas for more than twenty days, and the same immunity to motion sickness held true in his future voyages, no matter what the weather. It was a clear sign he was meant to be at sea, and for the next fifteen years that's just where he was, visiting far-flung places across the globe.

A couple of years after Jerry met Bob, Jerry was selling yachts in Charleston, South Carolina. When Bob visited him, a forty-one-foot Bavaria sailboat caught his eye, and he decided to buy it, naming it *At Ease.* The boat was a real beauty, with three cabins, two heads, European-style galley, salon with settee, bench seats, and large mahogany table, all illuminated by two deck skylights and hull ports. Unlike the *Almeisan,* the *At Ease* had an open cockpit without a hardtop or side curtains. Bob loved the boat, and the first person he invited on an extended sail was Jerry; together they sailed the *At Ease* north from Charleston, South Carolina, to Hampton Roads, Virginia, near where Bob was living at the time.

The voyage was a memorable one; they were hit by a sudden gale off Cape Hatteras, North Carolina, which hurled fifteen-foot confused seas at the *At Ease.* The boat proved a worthy match, performing exceptionally well, and Bob felt he received some invaluable on-the-job training from Jerry. The gale lasted about twelve hours, and when it subsided the two sailors enjoyed some exceptional sailing, as the *At Ease* flew up the coast in strong, steady winds.

Bob and Jerry worked so well together they decided to enter a sailing competition known as the Charleston to Bermuda Race, a 777-nautical mile voyage scheduled for May of 2005. Bob began the preparations by first scheduling time off from his piloting duties—no easy feat in the military. Next, he paid the entrance fee, and began making improvements to the *At Ease,* including repainting the boat's bottom, installing a new propeller, radios, spinnaker, and a life raft. All this work took twice as long as he expected, and he wasn't finished until just a few days before the start of the race.

Because Bob kept the boat moored outside Gloucester, Virginia, in Chesapeake Bay, he and Jerry first had to sail south to the race's starting point in Charleston. If they were to make it to Charleston in time for the race, they needed to set their departure date for Wednesday, May 4. Concerned over the weather forecast, Bob telephoned some of the National Weather Service contacts he'd gotten to know as a pilot. He learned that the predicted weather for late Thursday and Friday called for twenty- to thirty-knot winds with seas of seven to ten feet. The forecast reminded him of the conditions he and Jerry faced during their northbound trip when Bob first bought the boat, and he remembered that voyage as exhilarating but relatively safe. And so the two men decided to leave as planned but to keep an open mind about heading to the nearest port should forecasts deteriorate.

Without realizing it, Bob had made a decision to leave as scheduled that was similar to the mind-set that sometimes gets military pilots in trouble, a condition they call Get Homeitis: pilot talk referring to how pilots can sometimes become fixated on returning to base after a mission, no matter what the situation. In Bob's case with the *At Ease,* he had invested so much time and effort preparing for the race, all he wanted to do now was get started. It was a kind of reverse Get Homeitis, but equally as troublesome, because both scenarios focus exclusively on the goal and a schedule, without enough flexibility or consideration for variables. On the *Almeisan,* Tom Tighe had made a similar decision because he had a schedule to follow, especially with a new crew waiting in Bermuda for the return trip.

As Bob and Jerry sailed the *At Ease* out of Chesapeake Bay and turned south at Cape Henry, Virginia, the men enjoyed a bracing ride as strong winds sent the boat skimming speedily through lumbering five-foot swells. Both were happy to be back at sea, working as a team and seeing how well the vessel responded to their every command despite the high winds. In those first hours they enjoyed the very essence of sailing: the joy, freedom, and satisfaction of harnessing the power of the wind to seemingly fly over the ocean with no diesel engine to mar the sounds of the sea. Amazed at how the *At Ease* surged through the seas at seven knots, and even faster going down the backside of waves, Bob knew that the upgrades made to the boat were partly responsible, and he felt a heady mix of excitement and contentment.

Soon, however, the wind proved too strong and the men took in some sail. The seas grew to eight feet and the motion began to make Bob seasick, causing him to vomit over the side of the boat. Normally immune to seasickness, Bob became so nauseous and ill that over time his vomiting turned into violent dry heaves and he strained his esophagus and stomach. Jerry was feeling fine and he took the wheel, as conditions were too rough for the autopilot. Despite their foul-weather gear, both men were soon drenched and chilled in the open cockpit.

As nightfall cloaked the sailors in darkness, each man took a two-hour watch at the wheel. Bob was in a draining routine of finishing his watch, vomiting before he went below, struggling to remove his "foulies" and get into dry clothes, resting in his bunk, then, just before restorative sleep overtook him, getting dressed again to take the helm. The night hours crept by, and Jerry would ask Bob how he was holding up, reminding him to sip water to ward off dehydration. He offered to take longer watches, but Bob said he really couldn't sleep so he might as well make himself useful.

By morning the seas had grown to ten feet, and the two men discussed their options, including trying to sail to the closest port. After listening to an updated weather report the sailors calculated that they were seeing the worst of the storm, and that the whole mess would be past them within twenty-four hours, and they decided to press on so they wouldn't miss the start of the race. Bob thought his sea-sickness would soon be over, especially as he had endured so many stomach-turning maneuvers as a pilot with no ill effects.

The men slogged on through Thursday and continued pounding south as the second night closed in on them. They were now off Cape Hatteras, and with all its shoals, heading toward land was out of the question. The sailors could only go with the wind and head south.

Bob was still seasick, and of all the physical challenges he had faced in his life—including those in combat—this was the most demanding. But he gritted his teeth and resolved to fight through his exhaustion until they reached Charleston.

The seas were now twelve to fourteen feet, and steep, but this was about the maximum size that meteorologists predicted for their region. The *At Ease* still performed well, and when Friday morning dawned, both men figured conditions would turn for the better before the day was through.

In the early afternoon it appeared they were right: the clouds broke and sunlight glittered off the windswept seas. The sailors felt relief spread through their weary bodies, thinking that the wind would soon ease up. They were going to make it to Charleston with time to spare, which would be used to rest and regroup.

Or so they thought. Minutes later the clouds sealed shut as if someone had drawn a curtain, and it was clear the wind was not going to diminish. Bob and Jerry looked at each other, shaking their heads, resigned to the fact that they had only a few more hours of misery.

But this was no ordinary blow, for the monstrous low-pressure system was nowhere near its peak.

CHAPTER SIX

OFF THE EDGE OF A CLIFF

On board the *Almeisan* and *At Ease,* both crews are battered and exhausted, feeling as if they're in a fight with a heavyweight. The storm—their opponent—is absolutely ferocious and unrelenting. It cares nothing about the men and women in its path and has grown so large that even though the two boats are hundreds of miles apart, each crew assumes they're taking the worst the storm can throw at them. These assumptions are dead wrong.

The innermost section of the low-pressure system is now a tightly packed bomb, heading from south to north, hurling its strongest winds at the besieged boat off Cape Hatteras, the *At Ease.* The vessel is thirty miles offshore on the northern edge of the Gulf Stream, called the North Wall. The winds, which blast mostly from the northeast, are colliding with the north-flowing Gulf Stream, causing extra steep and viscous seas. The troughs are short between the waves, and only ten seconds pass between each strike. These are the worst kind of seas to be in; there is no gradual slope to climb up and over, only deep valleys and sheer mountains of water. Making matters worse, the breaking crests aren't just spilling down the face of the waves—they are suddenly and violently plunging, and the speed of the water in the "jet" of such a breaker can be up to four times faster than that of the wave itself.

Bob Cummings hasn't eaten a thing in two days, and although he's been sipping water he guesses he's dehydrated, adding to his weakness. The boat is rising and falling so wildly, so violently, and with such impact that his seasickness is getting worse instead of better. He's just gotten off watch, removed his foulies, and staggers into a bunk, when above the roar of the wind he hears a booming shout from the cockpit.

"Bob, I need you up here now!" Jerry yells.

Scrambling back into his foul-weather gear, Bob lurches to the companionway and scrambles up the steps out into the open air of the cockpit.

The waves have almost doubled in size, and Bob stares in stunned disbelief as thirty-foot monsters hurl themselves at the stern of the *At Ease,* which seems little more than a twig bobbing in the boiling waters. The full roar of the seas assaults Bob's ears, and he likens the sound to the revving engines of his Black Hawk chopper at take-off.

Each time a wave breaks on the stern of the *At Ease,* the boat accelerates so quickly that it broaches slightly on the downhill run. Now Bob realizes how apt the expression "angry seas" really is. All he can think is that the sea is actually chasing him, wanting to devour him, Jerry, and his beloved boat.

It takes Bob a moment to realize that Jerry is screaming at him. "Reef the sail! It's bloody hard to hold her!" Jerry's arms are aching from fighting the wheel, trying to keep the boat from broaching, but there's little response from his movement of the rudder because the boat is absolutely flying down the waves, sometimes hitting speeds of eighteen knots. To make matters worse, not all waves are coming out of the north. Some seas pummel the boat from the east and even the southeast, and there's no way for Jerry to anticipate where the next one will strike. Earlier he tried to heave to—a maneuver to change direction enough that the motion isn't as violent—but with no success.

Bob crouches in the cockpit and looks at the anemometer, which measures wind speed, and can't believe it's at its highest reading—sixty knots. Jerry shouts that the wind's velocity has increased so fast, there's no way he can get the sail down without someone at the wheel.

Bob manages to crawl out of the cockpit, where the wind tears at his skin and batters him with foam, spume, and spray. Somehow he furls the last remaining sail. When he crawls back into the cockpit, Jerry shouts, "Get your harness on and tether in!" Bob's heart skips a beat, thinking how he was just outside the cockpit without being tethered to the boat. He goes below, attaching his harness around his chest, but in his rush he can't find his inflatable personal flotation device (PFD).

Topside, tethered in, Bob realizes he's *underestimated* the size of the waves—some monsters loom over the boat a full thirty-five feet in height, their wind-streaked tops hurling down on the *At Ease*. The jagged crests look like teeth, and again Bob can't help but think the ocean is a living, breathing thing ready to bite down on him. It's hard for him to process everything that's happening. *Could the waves have grown an additional five feet in the last few minutes? If the anemometer is pegged at sixty, what is the real wind speed? Can this boat take much more? Can I? Can Jerry?*

Some of his questions will be answered swiftly, others a bit later, and some never. But we can get a glimpse into the true power of the winds via a recording taken by the Hyde County (North Carolina) Emergency Management Coordination Team, which measured one wind gust that evening at an incredible 115 miles per hour just off Cape Hatteras. If the anemometer on the *At Ease* could have recorded the true sustained wind speeds in excess of its maximum reading, it's a good bet that the blasts sweeping down on the boat top sixty-four knots, pushing this storm into force 12 on the Beaufort Scale—as high as the scale goes. At that level the winds are simply called hurricane force.

Dusk is closing in on the beleaguered sailors when Jerry shouts through the wind, "We should try letting her lie ahull!"

Lying ahull is a controversial topic among sailing experts. You give up control of the boat and consequently the vessel's bow no longer heads into the seas. You gamble that a massive broadside hit won't do you in. Most sailboats under bare poles and without engine power can ride the seas well—even sideways—so long as the swells are not extraordinarily steep or breaking.

Bob quickly agrees with Jerry's idea, and so the rudder is fixed to leeward, and in a tense moment they let go of the wheel and allow the bare-poled boat to ride the seas with no human guidance. The *At Ease* is now propelled sideways down the face of the waves with her port side low. Both men station themselves on the starboard side, with their backs to the oncoming waves, and say a silent prayer that this maneuver is the right one. There are few options left.

The first sideways ride down is terrifying and totally disorienting. As the boat hits the trough at a forty-five-degree angle it seems as if she will capsize.

Within minutes, however, it is clear to the sailors that despite the awkward plunging, the ride is actually a bit smoother. For a few moments the level of stress in both men dissipates a bit now that they are no longer fighting the sea. *Maybe this is what the ocean wanted us to do all along,* thinks Bob.

Just fifteen minutes later everything changes as a wave slides under the boat, and keeps on sliding so that the men rise so high above the trough it's like they are looking down from a skyscraper. Bob has the sensation the *At Ease* is being pulled up by a long tongue and into a set of jaws where it will be swallowed whole. Jerry is just watching in awe: *Thirty feet, forty feet, how much higher?* Having sailed more than 200,000 miles, he's seen a lot of waves, and as this wave reaches fifty feet in height, he thinks, *This is it, the boat can't stay upright.*

Next they hear an incredible thunderous sound, as the cresting fury of this enormous comber cascades down on them. There's no time to shout, no time even to turn around and face their attacker.

As the wave breaks directly over the men, sealing out the sky, they feel the boat drop out from under them. The *At Ease* is literally pushed by the breaking sea down the face of the wave in a free fall, and instead of having the vessel's mast above them, it is now below.

The roaring stops. All is deathly silent. Their world turns green-blue with bubbles everywhere. Both Bob and Jerry are underwater, and are not sure where they are in relation to the boat.

There are two kinds of knockdowns. The first, sometimes referred to as a B1, occurs when the sailboat goes over 90 degrees, stays there for a second or two, and then rights herself, hopefully with crewmembers still on board washed up against the lifelines or clinging desperately to the wheel in the cockpit. The second type, or a B2, is a whole lot worse. Here the sailboat suddenly rolls past 90 degrees, potentially all the way to 180 degrees, in a complete capsize, and holding onto a stanchion or the wheel is almost impossible.

Usually, the only thing that will keep a crew in an open cockpit from being snatched by the seas is their safety harness, which—God willing—has been properly secured to a section of the boat that does not break away.

The *At Ease* knockdown is a complete rollover, a 180-degree capsize, which many boats never recover from. Bob kicks to the surface, unable to understand immediately all that has happened in the chaos of battering seas. Then he sees a keel reaching skyward, and knows the boat is upside down. His thoughts become clearer: *You are tethered to a sinking boat. It will pull you under. You don't have a life jacket on.*

His hand reaches for the tether's safety catch. *Don't go down with the boat.* He wonders how long he can tread water as he floats next to the overturned boat.

Then a new voice whispers to him: *Bob, if you release from the boat you will die.*

He pauses, wondering where the words come from. But one thing is clear: the second voice, the one seemingly from somewhere outside of himself, is the right one, the one that wants him to live. Slowly, he moves his hand away from the safety release, and waits. Time stops.

Meanwhile Jerry is still holding onto the chrome bar above the binnacle. It's not even a conscious decision, but he clutches tightly in the turbulence. He's being shaken from side to side. Worried he'll be trapped under the boat, he too is ready to release his safety latch so that he can swim to the vessel's upwind side and avoid being crushed.

Then the boat rights itself. Jerry simply holds onto the binnacle bar and is brought up with the boat, still in the cockpit.

Bob is in the water looking up at the *At Ease,* wallowing five feet away. He's being dragged behind the boat. Should the tether snap, Bob will be engulfed by the raging seas and disappear into the void of endless ocean.

And now Jerry is in the stern of the cockpit reaching over the rail toward Bob, who has pulled himself along his tether to within a foot of the vessel. Bob grabs hold of the stern rail, and Jerry reaches down, grabs Bob by the collar of his fleece jacket, and helps pull him back aboard.

As Bob collapses into the cockpit, he experiences a surreal feeling about his brush with death, and can't help but think of the old military saying, "Emergency procedures are written in blood." *How true.*

Suddenly he is jolted from this thought as he looks over the stern of the boat in stunned disbelief. The life raft, still in its canister, is floating behind the boat, connected by a long tether. The men try to pull it back to the vessel, but it's no use, and they tie the tether off, hoping the raft won't inflate and praying it won't get ripped away entirely. Bob thinks it's only a matter of time before one or both of those scenarios happen in the face of such murderous seas.

Now that lying ahull has proved to be disastrous, the men decide to start the engine and try to get their bow back into the seas. The engine starts with a comforting muffled roar, then sputters and dies. Lines from the boat might be fouled in the prop. They try to clear the lines, but each time they start the engine it quits as soon as they try to put it in gear to engage the propeller. Jerry thinks the shaft going to the propeller is cracked, but whatever the reason, the propeller won't turn. They finally give up the idea of motoring into the seas, and instead start the engine, and leave it in neutral; this way at least it will power the batteries, which in turn will power the radio, lights, and pump.

They consider trying to raise a bit of sail, but realize the winch handles are gone. Earlier, in a safety-conscious effort, they removed the handles, worried that if one of them fell on the protruding levers they'd risk serious injury. And so the handles were removed and placed in a bag. But of course when the boat capsized, the bag of handles was the first thing to be swept away.

The men are nervous that they are being blown too near the coast, with its myriad of shoals, but they are unable to maneuver the boat. This is when they agree to radio the Coast Guard of their position and inform them of the situation. It's not a Mayday, but their predicament is bad enough that they want the Coast Guard to be aware of their plight, and the two sailors agree to keep the Coast Guard updated.

There's nothing more the men can do in the cockpit, and the danger of being knocked overboard again is real. Going belowdecks seems safer, although both men know that if the *At Ease* rolls again, and this time doesn't come up, they will likely be trapped and that will be the end. Still, they dog down the companionway hatch, sealing themselves in the belly of the boat. The galley and salon are in total shambles, with gear, supplies, and seawater sloshing about the port side because of the list. Making matters even more dangerous, a bottle of olive oil has shattered, transforming the cabin sole (floor) into an ice skating rink, adding to the chaos.

They notice that a Lexan porthole is broken and water continues to splash in through the opening. Quickly the two men stuff a cushion in the hole, then lay a piece of plywood over it, screwing it in place.

Bob shakes his head, sickened by the destruction around him.

But Jerry wants Bob to view the whole picture. "Bob," he says, "look past the mess. Just look at the boat itself. We're still in good shape."

Bob nods, but he feels his body crashing from the killer combination of sleep deprivation and two days of seasickness. He needs to lie down, and is thankful Jerry can take over the decision making while he rests. He wants to catch his breath for a moment, think things through. He's been in situations in the military where he could have died, and he knows the feeling. This is one of those situations. First they must bail out the vessel as best they can with a small hand pump. When they have emptied as much water as possible, Bob finally places cushions on the soggy sole boards and lies down, every muscle in his body fatigued and hurting.

The boat continues its wild ride, surfing sideways down the face of the waves. The fate of the two mariners now rests in the integrity of the vessel.

CHAPTER SEVEN

"SET OFF YOUR EPIRB!"

As the night progresses Jerry perches on one of the upper steps of the companionway ladder, smoking a cigarette, wondering what's going to happen next. He's got his back against one side of the wall and his feet pressing against the opposite side, so that he's wedged firmly. The hatch is made out of clear Lexan and Jerry can watch the foam and seas wash over it, as if probing for a way to get inside. Every now and again a big wave slams into the *At Ease,* and it heels over forty-five degrees, and Jerry holds on tight to the rail along the ladder's edge to keep from being thrown below. In the gloom of night, all his senses are heightened, and he feels just how strong the waves are as they bang on the hull, making the boat creak and shudder. In between the big hits, various grim scenarios and the final outcome flash through Jerry's mind. He thinks the chances of the boat's making it through the storm in one piece are slim. Having been in several storms in his many transatlantic voyages, he can't help but try to compare them to this nightmare. But they really don't measure up: he's never had a fifty-foot wave engulf his boat and he's never experienced a complete knockdown and been held underwater. And now, sealed inside the *At Ease* with no way to motor or steer her, he wonders if this will be his coffin, thinking that it's just a matter of time before the boat capsizes again.

Around 11 p.m., Bob wakes from his fitful sleep and carefully walks to Jerry, intending to let him get some rest.

"You OK?" Bob asks.

"Bob," Jerry says, "we've got to talk. This storm has not eased up, it might have even gotten worse." Jerry pauses and looks Bob in the eye. "We should consider calling a Mayday."

37

Bob doesn't answer right away. Outside the seas thunder in the coal black night, shaking the boat as a cat would a mouse.

"I don't think so," says Bob slowly. "It's just too dangerous for the pilots to come into this mess at night. I can't risk having anyone lose their life when we still have a chance to hang on till morning."

Jerry smiles. "You know pilots. Let's sit tight." Jerry thinks to himself, *It's bloody amazing he's still on the ball, still weighing all the factors, still thinking of others.* Five minutes later, as if to mock Bob's decision not to call for help, the seas blow out the plywood patch of wood mounted over the broken porthole and the ocean pours through. The two men scramble to repair it before more water cascades in. When the job is done Bob realizes that he's actually over his seasickness.

Despite being knocked around like a Ping-Pong ball, Bob finally falls into a deep sleep around 12:30 a.m. Saturday morning. He's still on cushions on the sole boards with his feet up against the bulkhead to the head, which is on the port side. This keeps him from rolling each time the boat heels as it slides sideways down the waves. Every now and then a giant sea staggers the crippled vessel, causing Bob to wake, and it takes a second for him to realize where he is and that this nightmare is for real. But the *At Ease* always manages to return upright from the wallops, and Bob falls back asleep, knowing there's nothing he can do.

Jerry is trying to rest as well. Earlier he used the bilge pump, located at the boat's center, in an effort to remove some of the water sloshing around. But because the *At Ease* has a shallow bilge, and most of the water has collected on the port side, the pump is largely ineffective. Every hour Jerry calls the Coast Guard to keep them abreast of the situation.

Now Jerry's just looking forward to dawn. He figures once he can see the waves approaching he'll be better off in the cockpit, and maybe it will be more conducive for trying to heave to or deploying a drogue, a parachute-shaped device that is trailed from the stern to create drag and slow the boat in heavy weather. In the meantime, he's resumed his balancing act on the companionway stairs, almost mesmerized by the water sliding over the clear hatchway above him. He glances down and notices a bottle of Yuengling beer floating in the water. *God damn it, I'm going to have a beer.* He snatches the bottle out of the sloshing seawater, and returns to his perch. *Bloody hell, this may be my last beer, might as well enjoy it.* He taps a cigarette from his pack, lights it, and enjoys a long leisurely smoke with his beer.

Bob happens to wake, opens his eyes, and the first thing he sees is Jerry sipping his beer and casually blowing smoke after a long, deep pull on his cigarette. "I can't believe it," says Bob, "you're absolutely mad." Then Bob falls right back to sleep.

Jerry smiles, and nods his head.

Another hour goes by and Jerry realizes he's not accomplishing anything by being awake. He calls the Coast Guard to give them the periodic update, telling them their situation is the same. Then he spreads cushions on the sole boards, lies down, and blissful sleep overtakes him immediately.

It's now 5:30 a.m., and the center of the low-pressure system has surged by the *At Ease* and is located to the northeast so that its counterclockwise-spinning winds are now striking the boat from the northwest. Waves, however, still batter the vessel from different angles, making it impossible to predict exactly how or when the boat will lurch at the next impact, but, remarkably, both men are still asleep.

Just as it looks as if they will make it to daylight, the most massive wave of all comes lumbering toward the unsuspecting men. *Bang!* The impact sounds as if they've been hit by a train. The *At Ease* is slammed so hard that she can't recover, and over she heels, throwing both men into the air.

Bob finds that his hands and knees are on the overhead (ceiling), which is now mostly below him, and he immediately realizes the boat is upside down.

Jerry is thrown off the floor not knowing which way is up. A brief flare of panic surges through him, *Holy shit, this could be it!* He glances to his left and realizes he's looking at the overhead, which means he's lying on the port-side wall. The panic is replaced by adrenaline; he jumps to his feet, thinking, *Another knockdown!* He looks up the companionway ladder. Torrents of green water avalanche down the steps, charging at the men.

39

The companionway hatch is gone and there's nothing to stop the sea.

It flashes through the minds of both men that in the next seconds their fates will be determined. With the boat capsized and the seas flooding her, there is little hope for escape if she doesn't recover. The *At Ease* is in the trough of a wave, and the roaring sound stops for a moment. Ever so slowly, Bob and Jerry feel their boat struggling to right itself, as if it too has a mind of its own and is determined to continue the fight and reach for the air. First they sense the boat is at ninety degrees, and then they feel the weight of the keel lowering the hull while the deck rises free of the writhing sea, breaking the surface.

The *At Ease* now has two holes in her, and if she gets knocked down again with so much water in her, chances are she's not coming up.

Bob takes one look around, and realizes just how dire their predicament is. "Jerry!" he shouts, "set off your EPIRB!"

Jerry has his own personal EPIRB (Emergency Position Indicating Radio Beacon) and immediately activates it. Bob does the same with the EPIRB always carried on the boat.

Jerry half swims, half runs toward the companionway and climbs into the cockpit, surprised that all his limbs are still working. He takes a quick look around for the companionway hatch, but it's been swept away. He then holds his yellow EPIRB high, wanting to make sure the signal has a clear shot to satellites above. Next, he ducks back below and wades to his berth, where he pulls out his passport, green card, and wallet, and stashes those, together with his cigarettes and lighter, into a waterproof pouch and secures it around his neck.

Bob does the same with his valuables, but then stops, alarmed by a smell of something burning. Rushing back to the salon he sees a thin stream of blue-gray smoke drifting from the electrical panel, which is on the port side and had been submerged in the knockdown. Bob's worried the panel will ignite because the fuse has not burnt out and the batteries are still sending power to the panel. As he reaches to get the bolt off the fuse panel so that he can disconnect the cable, a painful shock charges through his hand and up his arm. He jumps back, shaking his arm in pain. Then he tries again. He's more wor-

The *At Ease*

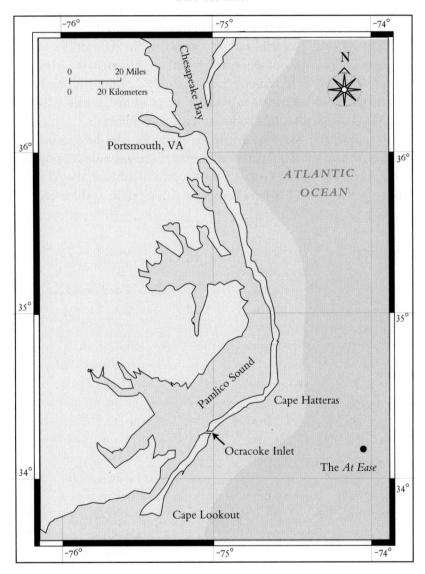

The *At Ease* was off Cape Hatteras in the middle of the Gulf Stream when Captain Bob Cummings set off the EPIRB.

ried about the vessel going up in flames than about the shocks. He manages to get the cable free, but smoke is still wafting out of the electrical panel.

Bob feels there's not much time before flames erupt, and he runs to the boat's main batteries and disconnects them. The smoke stops. But now the radio won't work, and he needs to broadcast a Mayday. He hotwires the VHF radio, bypassing the DC panel, and the radio powers up. Then, as calmly as possible, he picks up the mike: "Mayday, Mayday, Mayday, this is the sailing vessel *At Ease.*"

He repeats the Mayday, giving his position. Minutes go by and there is no answer. The men realize why no response comes on the radio. They are out of range of the Coast Guard base they'd been talking with earlier. They are completely alone now, at the mercy of the sea.

CHAPTER EIGHT

A RESCUE SWIMMER'S NIGHTMARE

At the U.S. Coast Guard Search and Rescue Command Center in Portsmouth, Virginia, both EPIRB signals from the *At Ease* are heard loud and clear. Each EPIRB had been registered with the Coast Guard when it was first purchased, and the number on the EPIRB could be traced back to the owner, who had supplied contact telephone numbers.

A Coast Guard radio operator calls the contact number listed with Jerry's EPIRB, and wakes up Jerry's wife, Leah, saying, "Jerry McCarthy's EPIRB has gone off. May we talk to him?"

"Jerry's at sea," Leah anxiously answers. "If his EPIRB has gone off that means he's using it on the boat and he's in real trouble. He's an experienced sailor, so something must be terribly wrong."

Seconds after the phone call, a ship's captain at sea radios the Coast Guard that he has just heard a Mayday from a sailing vessel called the *At Ease,* confirming the sailboat is in a desperate situation. Lieutenant Libby Pruitt and Petty Officer Matt Doscher at the command center immediately direct a C-130 search plane, stationed at U.S. Coast Guard Air Station Elizabeth City, North Carolina, to fly to *At Ease.* The C-130, a four-engine turboprop fixed-wing aircraft, is a workhorse for the Coast Guard because of its versatility and long-range flying capability.

At Air Station Elizabeth City, the search and rescue alarm sounds, rousing not only the C-130 crew but also the other Coasties at the station, including twenty-one-year-old rescue swimmer Jeremiah Loser. "I got up," says Jeremiah, "because I figured if the C-130 was launched, we might be next. I went down to flight operations, and sure enough, a half hour later at about six thirty a.m., I learned our helicopter team was also going."

Helicopter pilots Lieutenant Commander Dan Molthen and Lieutenant Andy Barrow jump into their flight suits and race to their aircraft. Mechanic Randy Swanz stands outside the aircraft, clearing the area, as the pilots warm up the helicopter. As Swanz boards the helo, Jeremiah comes running, clutching all his gear, and joins the others on the HH-60 Jayhawk helicopter, now ready to go. Within minutes the four men are airborne, but just seconds later serious problems crop up. First their radar goes out, then the GPS dies, and the high-tech helicopter is basically being navigated by eight sets of eyeballs. After many attempts to fix the electronics, flight commander Molthen decides to abort the flight and they are back on the ground at Elizabeth City within twenty minutes. Another helicopter is waiting, and the four men sprint to it, hoping the aircraft works as advertised.

The second Jayhawk is aloft within ten minutes, and the crew flies southeast, buffeted by fifty- to sixty-knot wind blasts. The winds are of concern, but the crew knows they're lucky that the sun has just come up—there are few rescues more dangerous than trying to airlift sailors off a sailboat at night, especially because of the boat's tall mast rising and plunging with the waves.

"At that time, all we know about the Mayday," recalls Jeremiah, "is that a sailboat is taking on water and the crew is in danger. I can see how big the waves are, so I figure I'm going to need all the energy I can get. We have some box lunches on board and before seven thirty a.m., I'd already eaten two of them." He also knows that on rare occasions rescue swimmers can get left in the water for a few more hours than expected, so he wants to have plenty of fuel in his tank just in case.

On board the *At Ease,* Bob and Jerry are relieved that a ship has acknowledged their Mayday and passed it on to the Coast Guard. Now it's a waiting game. Can the Coast Guard arrive before another knockdown? The boat's dead in the water—a sitting duck for whatever the sea has in store for them. Jerry and Bob, however, don't want to be passive victims, so they use buckets to bail water, which is now two feet deep on the port side of the cabin.

Dawn has broken, and Bob takes solace knowing that the Coast

Guard helicopter pilots will have light to see by, and the clouds are dissipating. Occasionally one of the men goes up into the cockpit to have a look around, but there's little to see except the endless advance of wind-streaked waves. And when the boat careens down into a trough, their view of the horizon is entirely cut off and they can only look up to where the wave tops reach toward the gray sky. Neither man stays in the cockpit for long, aware of the danger of being swept over.

At 8:30 a.m. the two sailors hear the C-130 and scramble topside. They look skyward and the plane swoops down directly overhead, waving its wings, letting the men know they have been seen.

Jerry pumps his fist and shouts, "Yes! They've found us!" Pure joy surges through his body—he no longer feels like a little speck in the void. Somebody knows exactly where he and Bob are.

Bob is able to make radio contact with the plane's pilots, and answers their questions about the number of people on board the vessel, what they are wearing, whether they have personal flotation devices on, and the latest status of the boat. The plane then makes slow sweeping circles around the boat, keeping them in constant sight.

A half hour later Bob and Jerry first hear, then see, the helicopter. They make radio contact, and pilot Andy Barrow explains that they are going to drop a rescue swimmer in the ocean, and that when he reaches the stern of the *At Ease* they should follow his orders.

Jeremiah looks down at the wildly heaving boat, noting that the waves are "totally pummeling the vessel." The four men in the aircraft use their headsets to discuss the best place to lower Jeremiah, finally agreeing to drop him in front of the sailboat, and let the wind and waves bring him back to the boat.

"I go down on the hook," explains Jeremiah, "and as soon as I disconnect, the boat is nearly on top of me, it's moving that fast. To avoid being crushed, I swim as fast as I can to the left."

Bob watches in amazement, impressed at the way the swimmer knifes through the water, and well aware that their rescuer is all alone in the giant swells, taking an incredible risk.

Jeremiah notices that lines are trailing off the stern, and he grabs one, thinking he can pull himself to the vessel. Instead he becomes entangled in the lines and is being dragged behind the boat—sideways—ingesting a considerable amount of seawater. Fortunately he has a knife strapped to his waist and he uses it to cut himself free. Now about twenty-five feet behind the boat, he again grabs a trailing line, and this time is able to slowly pull himself hand over hand toward the sailboat. In his dry suit, he's sweating like crazy, feeling as if he's doing nonstop push-ups.

After several minutes he makes it to the stern of the *At Ease* and clutches onto a small hanging ladder that Bob has lowered, then starts to climb. A thirty-five-foot wave, however, lifts the boat up, bringing Jeremiah completely out of the water, and then slams him back down, submerging him. He's still hanging onto the ladder, and he manages to climb another rung before the next wave repeats the process. This time Jeremiah's hand is caught behind the ladder, and when the wave drops out from under him his hand is crushed between the ladder and the boat. The pain is so intense he wonders if his hand is broken, but he doggedly clings onto the ladder. Jerry and Bob try to pull him aboard but the violent seas make it impossible.

Jeremiah removes his snorkel, and shouts to the men, "Forget getting me on board! I'm going to have each of you jump off one at a time. Leave everything behind except your wallets! Don't jump until I tell you!" He catches his breath as the boat continues to catapult him up then slam him down with each passing wave. Then he looks at Jerry. "You're going to be first. When I say jump, you jump immediately, and I'll grab you! Just float along with me and I'll get you in the rescue basket!"

Jerry turns to Bob and says, "See you up there, mate." He then tightens his life jacket, and double checks to make sure his EPIRB is attached to him in case he falls out of the basket and gets separated from the rescue swimmer.

Jeremiah shouts, "OK, jump, now!"

And Jerry leaps into the gray-green seas.

Jeremiah quickly swims to Jerry and gets behind and underneath him, in what is called the "buddy float." By the time Jeremiah signals toward the helicopter to lower the basket, the *At Ease* has already been blown out of sight.

With Jeremiah's help, Jerry is in the basket and lifted into the helicopter. Inside the chopper it's so loud Jerry can't hear a thing, and the hoist operator hands him earplugs. One of the pilots turns around and gives Jerry a thumbs-up and Jerry does the same. Jerry looks down at the seas and the drifting *At Ease,* getting a whole new perspective on just how big the waves are. The sailboat looks like a child's toy among the oncoming seas.

Jeremiah is treading water below, now feeling the full effects of his nonstop exertion. He wishes he were in a wet suit rather than a dry suit, because the ocean temperature is about 70 degrees, and he's boiling inside its confines. The *At Ease* is already more than a thousand yards away, and Jeremiah signals the hoist operator to lower the basket again—he needs to be carried closer to the sailboat.

Bob, alone on the boat, takes this opportunity to shut off all power on the *At Ease.* He doesn't want the boat to catch fire and potentially have a passing ship see the smoke and think there is another emergency.

When the helicopter is in a 100-foot hover in front of the boat, Jeremiah jumps in the water, swims to the *At Ease* transom, and motions Bob to jump. He's able to get Bob into the basket quickly, but two large waves totally bury Jeremiah, and he takes in more seawater. When he kicks to the surface he looks up and sees with satisfaction that Bob is being pulled into the helicopter.

Jeremiah vomits, totally spent, barely able to move his leaden arms or his bruised, throbbing right hand. As the bare hook is lowered by the flight mechanic, Jeremiah struggles toward it, but his arms are just slapping the ocean's surface. A wave crashes down on him, burying him beneath white water. When he surfaces, he's no closer to the hook. He's so tired that he thinks, *Don't worry about the hook, you need to rest.* This is followed by a realization that screams at his very being: *If you don't get that hook, it's all over!*

He kicks as hard as he can, and wills his arms to stroke for just one more minute. This last effort brings him to the hook and he clips on, then slumps over, panting and straining to get more air in his lungs. He manages to raise his arm, signaling to the hoist operator to winch him up. Nothing happens.

A wave picks him up, and then as it drops away beneath him he free-falls a few feet before the cable abruptly jerks him to a stop, his full body weight straining against the harness as he hangs in midair. Over the next minute, four more waves lift him up, only to slide away and send him plunging before yanking him at the end of the cable, several feet above the wave trough. The twenty-one-year-old wonders how much more he can take before he passes out.

Above, in the helicopter, the cable is jammed, and mechanic and hoist operator Randy Swanz is furiously trying to free it. When he completes the task he winches Jeremiah up, terrified for his friend.

"You all right?" Randy shouts.

Jeremiah is so winded he can't talk, and he nods, signaling with his hand that he needs a minute to catch his breath. Randy holds out a bottle of water, and after a few seconds Jeremiah takes a swig.

Lieutenant Commander Molthen looks back from the instruments with concern. "You OK?"

Jeremiah has caught his breath. "I'm fine, sir. Just needed some water."

Molthen makes sure everyone is strapped in.

Before the cabin door is closed, Bob Cummings looks down at a heartbreaking scene: the *At Ease* is drifting away in the giant swells.

Later, when Jerry is back at home, the phone rings, and he answers the call. His mother is calling from Ireland and before Jerry even mentions the accident, his mother says, "Thank God you're all right, thank God the Coast Guard found you."

Jerry is stunned that his mother knows what happened. "How did you know I was in trouble?" he asks.

Mrs. McCarthy explains that she had a dream the previous night about Jerry being out at sea and being tossed about by huge seas and ferocious winds. "Even when I woke up I couldn't shake the feeling that something was wrong," says Mrs. McCarthy, "but I told myself it was only a silly dream, and I went about my business trying to shake this feeling of dread."

Mrs. McCarthy goes on to say that a few hours later she was watching Sky TV and her heart skipped a beat. A reporter started to detail how a storm off the east coast of the United States had put several boats in jeopardy. The reporter added, "One of the boats is said to be the *At Ease,* crewed by Robert Cummings and Jerry McCarthy."

"Oh my God!" shouted Mrs. McCarthy, "that's Jerry, that's my son!" Mrs. McCarthy then called the Irish Coast Guard, explaining that it was her son mentioned in the news report. The Irish Coast Guard then contacted the USCG in Elizabeth City, North Carolina, and patched them through to Mrs. McCarthy. Incredibly, she was connected to one of Jerry's rescuers, who said, "That was your son and he's fine."

Whether Mrs. McCarthy had a premonition or mother's intuition or coincidental dream can't be known for sure, but whatever she experienced was accurate. The final outcome was all that mattered: her son was safe from the rampaging seas.

There is, however, one last boat caught in clutches of the storm, the *Almeisan,* and its occupants are anything but safe.

PART II

CHAPTER NINE

THROUGH THE GULF STREAM

While Bob Cummings and Jerry McCarthy are being whisked away by the Coast Guard helicopter toward land and safety, the crew of the *Almeisan* is growing increasingly concerned over the deteriorating conditions. Updated weather reports are only adding to their anxiety, predicting that the low-pressure system will both deepen and expand more than previously forecast.

The sailors have been unable to cross the Gulf Stream—only thirty miles away—because the winds are coming directly out of the east, making it impossible to turn into the giant waves bulldozing at the boat. Captain Tighe has only one option, and that is to motor due south, paralleling the Gulf Stream, and wait for a shift in the winds. When he gets the chance, he wants to cross the Gulf Stream at a sharp angle of almost ninety degrees, so that its northeasterly currents don't push them farther from Bermuda. The combers average twelve feet in height, but every now and then a sinister-looking wave a bit steeper than the others bears down on the boat, rattling the crew's nerves with a large bang. Should they need to be rescued, they are in perhaps the worst possible place: more than 250 miles from the U.S. mainland, and still 300 miles from Bermuda.

Loch and Kathy are on watch, but they can't see very much. With such high seas and wind-whipped rain, visibility is poor, and the watch-standers wouldn't see another boat or ship until it was virtually on top of them. Chris, the first victim of the insidious seasickness, has been lying on the cockpit floor most of the night, but now, at 9 a.m. on Saturday, he is finally starting to feel better. Despite his exhaustion he's in awe of the size, and even the majesty, of the giant rollers surrounding the *Almeisan*. The sky adds more drama to the scene, briefly clearing so that rainbows form, disappear, then re-form. And with the additional light, the color of the ocean loses its drab gray hue and is the deepest shade of blue Chris has ever seen.

A few minutes later the dark clouds are back and Chris notices that the anchor is starting to come loose and informs Tom, offering to go out on deck and secure it. Tom, however, says he'll do it, as he's worried it is too dangerous to send Chris on deck. To be on the safe side, Tom dons a survival suit, and when he exits the cockpit the first thing he does is clip his lifeline to the jackline that runs the entire length of the boat on deck. Screaming wind tears at his face and the rain pelts him relentlessly, making it difficult to see. Nevertheless, he fights his way to the bow, secures the anchor and then carefully, in a crouching walk, returns to the cabin.

With each hour, the exhausted and sleep-deprived captain is moving more slowly, and talking less. A hundred thoughts are racing through his mind, but there's not much he can do until the storm passes. As if to hurl an insult, an occasional wave hits the boat on the beam, sending a shudder through the *Almeisan.*

Later in the morning, Tom and Loch raise the mizzen sail and fisherman sail to attempt tacking into the wind. But no matter what maneuver they try, nothing works. They also realize that the autopilot is overreacting to the pitch and roll of the boat, so they turn it off for good and steer manually. Not long afterward they take down both sails, but continue under engine power.

Like Chris, Ron is feeling a bit better, and although still queasy he comes into the cockpit to give Kathy, Loch, and Tom a break. He and Chris stand watch. They now notice that the seas are streaked with white foam where the wind has sheared the crests off waves. Just minutes into their watch, the storm makes its first direct assault on the *Almeisan,* like a fighter who flicks a painful jab at his opponent, testing, taunting. A huge wave of perhaps twenty feet hits the vessel from a slightly different direction, staggering the sailboat with a loud roar while tearing a section of curtain in the cockpit and drenching the two men. Water cascades down the companionway, setting off the bilge alarm, which goes off in the presence of water, and the sudden sound frays the nerves of everyone.

Some old-time sailors call these waves "queer seas," while another might say it is a mini rogue wave or a "freaker," but whatever the name, it catches the crew off guard. They have just gone through thousands of waves all about the same size, and then this sea hits them out of left field. Whatever comfort they felt from the uniformity of the waves is gone, replaced by the knowledge that the sea can, and will, do the unexpected. Chris and Ron exchange glances, knowing that the ocean, and not the man on the wheel, now controls what the boat does next.

Tom struggles up from below, making sure the watch-standers are safe, shaking his head as he looks at the torn curtains in the cockpit. "That's never happened before," he says softly. He asks Ron and Chris to use wire to repair the curtain, while he heads back below to get the boat pumped out.

Loch joins Tom, and tells him that he was lying down when the wave hit and the force of the water sent spray through a porthole. He thought the porthole wasn't secured properly, but when he went to tighten it he realized it was dogged down all the way. Both men shake their heads; the *Almeisan* is a tough boat, but that means nothing in this storm.

The engine power seems to have little effect in the growing seas, and Tom decides to lie ahull, turning off the engine and letting the boat simply ride the waves. He knows all too well that the ocean is calling the shots, and he and Loch—just like Bob Cummings and Jerry McCarthy—decide it's best not to fight it. When the wind direction changes, Tom will reassess the situation.

Lying ahull, however, has its own dangers. The waves coming at the *Almeisan* are growing in size, becoming more precipitous, and occasionally the very tops are collapsing. In these conditions some skippers would never lie ahull. Others would answer that there is no perfect solution; each boat, each situation, is different, and only the captain in the fight, in the maelstrom, can judge how best to ride the gale out.

As Saturday afternoon fades toward evening, Tom and Loch finally have some good news to celebrate; the winds have shifted a bit, pushing the *Almeisan* east-southeastward, and soon they enter the Gulf Stream. Loch also thinks to himself that should anything go wrong, at least they will be in warm water. He keeps the thought to himself but suspects Tom has the same idea. The *Almeisan* is drifting and surfing a bit less violently, heading in the right direction, and the sailors decide to let the vessel continue to lie ahull.

Loch and Tom are relieved to have reached the meandering waters of the Gulf Stream, but it won't help alleviate the howling gale they are in, and may actually make the air more unstable. Air warmed by the Gulf Stream carries its heat and water vapor aloft, colliding with colder air, which aids in the formation of thunderstorm cells, unpredictable winds, and even water spouts. The *Almeisan* and Tom Tighe have already experienced the heaviest weather of any of their previous forty-eight trips to Bermuda; both are at their limits, and certainly need no surprises.

Ron Burd is grateful he's been able to stand watch and spell Kathy, Tom, and Loch. He's feeling better, but is slow to recover his usual energy, and needs to rest when his watch is over. Heading below, he lies on the settee in the galley, hoping the rolling, rising, and falling of the boat do not induce another bout of seasickness. He's just closed his eyes when suddenly he feels himself being thrown through the air, stopping only when his forehead smacks into the chart table, snapping the table's wooden legs and sending shards of wood in all directions. Staggering to his feet, Ron knows the ocean just threw another surprise punch, and he wonders about the damage up above. He begins to climb the companionway, but he's disoriented and lightheaded and has to sit down before he loses consciousness. Running his hand along his forehead, he feels an egg-size contusion jutting out from his skull.

Kathy has heard the crash in the galley, and goes to Ron's aid, helping him to his feet and walking him back to the settee. She gets ice from the refrigerator and applies it to his bruise. Tom and Loch check on Ron and have him lie still, worrying about a concussion. They then set about dissembling the broken chart table so no one will bump into its jagged edge. Chris is above standing watch, wondering when the next surprise wave will hit.

Ron is lucky—he does not show any of the symptoms of concussion nor does the wound open and bleed. He just feels a bone-crushing weariness, probably as much from being seasick as from his collision with the chart table.

The rest of the crew isn't in much better shape than Ron, but Tom is already thinking ahead, and talks to Loch about repairs that will need to be made in Bermuda. He tells Loch he will postpone the return trip until the boat is shipshape, and he asks his friend if he will make the return trip with him. Loch says of course. He feels for the skipper and can sense the pressure Tom is putting on himself, worrying about the crew, knowing they all wish they were anywhere but here.

Not long after cleaning up the chart table, Loch loses his battle with the nauseous feeling he's been fighting, and he gets sick in earnest, vomiting, then being racked with dry heaves. He crawls into his aft cabin and shuts his eyes, hoping that will help the dizziness. Like the others, Loch is not prone to seasickness, but he's never been in seas this big. The waves are approximately fifteen feet in height now, and the *Almeisan* pitches and rolls like a leaf being hurled down a chute of rapids on a river.

Later, Tom checks in on Loch and offers some comforting words. Loch sees the stress and exhaustion etched in Tom's face, and jokes, "Some first mate I am. You would think it's my first trip." Tom tells him to get some rest, and Loch responds by trying to cheer his skipper, saying, "You picked a good crew. They are all doing great, and nobody's complaining." Tom nods, and with heavy, methodical steps carefully heads back up to the cockpit, reluctant to rest with the storm still raging. He just wants this nightmare to end, but the storm is far from finished, and in fact is still gathering strength.

CHAPTER TEN

KNOCKDOWN!

Although the crew does not know it yet, the storm's path has veered from due north to a more northeasterly trajectory, and the center of the low is not far from the *Almeisan*. Storms sometimes make unpredictable moves, and this is one of them. Occasionally the center of a low-pressure system wobbles or stalls, and in other instances, like this one, veers off from the direction previously followed. The rain is inconsistent as well, usually so intense it's as if someone is spilling a giant bucket of water on the drifting sailboat, but now and then it eases so that the cacophonous drumming on the boat's hardtop falls to a patter. The one constant is the wind: the crew hears it howl in all its blasting fury each time the boat is lifted out of a trough and toward the crest of a wave. The wind often catches the shrouds and riggings in such a way that the sound is shrill and high-pitched. Sometimes the boat teeters sickeningly at the top of the precipitous crests, and whoever is on watch braces himself and clenches his teeth before the wave passes beneath and the boat races down its back side before wallowing in the trough.

Earlier, both Ron and Chris had asked Tom about deploying a drogue, but learned there was none on board. The drogue is designed to trail behind the boat under the water's surface, slowing the vessel as it careens down waves. It adds a bit of stability so the vessel won't turn sideways and broach as the wave propels it forward. In all of Tom's many voyages to Bermuda, he's always been able to sail the boat through angry seas and has never had to use a drogue; consequently this piece of equipment is now packed away at home in his garage.

By 7:30 p.m. darkness has enveloped the *Almeisan,* and Chris tentatively tries his first food, macaroni and cheese, since becoming seasick forty-eight hours earlier. Then he rejoins Ron in the cockpit for watch duty. In the darkened cockpit they say little. As they endure the onslaught of angry seas, each man wonders if the storm is at or near its peak, hoping they have been through the worst of it.

Just before 11 p.m., Loch forces himself out of his bunk and carefully, using every handhold possible, makes his way toward the cockpit. Still weak and queasy, he's hoping that maybe by moving and helping the crew, he will feel better. He notices that the sliding hatchway at the top of the companionway has been dogged down, so that spray entering the cockpit won't run down below. He unfastens the hatchway, slides the panels to the side, and climbs the ladder into the cockpit, where he immediately clips his safety tether to a corner pad-eye (a metal ring usually used to secure sailing lines). The rest of the crew is already there, all in foul-weather gear and life jackets, and barely visible in the coal black night, with the only illumination coming from the instrument panels and compass. It's an eerie and disconcerting scene, especially with the humming in the wire rigging, a strange pitch unlike anything Loch has ever heard.

Kathy has just made an entry in the logbook, recording that the barometer is 28.3, air temperature 63 Fahrenheit, water temperature 75 Fahrenheit, wind at 41 knots, seas 18–20 feet. And based on what Tom has told her of the latest weather forecast she adds, "Gale force continues, but optimistic forecast for the morning."

Chris and Ron ask Loch how he's feeling, knowing all too well the utter fatigue caused by seasickness. They also say the *Almeisan* has been handling as well as can be expected during the last couple of hours, and then they head below for some rest, leaving Loch, Kathy, and Tom sitting in the cockpit.

Chris has not been in his bunk since he became seasick two days earlier, and he looks forward to lying down on something softer than the deck of the cockpit. Reaching his cabin, he removes his foul-weather gear and life jacket and puts on a pair of pajama bottoms. Still worried about seasickness, he decides the center of the boat would be a bit more stable than his forward cabin, and stumbles back to the salon. The L-shaped settee with its cushions looks inviting, and Chris lies down on it with his head in the corner where the two benches meet, and his feet toward the centerline. Above him are the angled, forward-facing windows, approximately two feet by five.

Chris's head keeps hitting the settee backrest each time the boat heels, and he struggles back upright and changes his position, lying down on the fore-aft portion of the settee so that his head is well aft of the windows and his feet are back in the corner where his head had previously been.

This simple shift will save Chris's life.

In the early morning hours of Sunday, May 8, the seas rapidly grow from twenty feet to thirty feet, and the hull of the *Almeisan* takes a pounding like never before. Ron and Chris, exhausted from their earlier seasickness, somehow manage to sleep through the beating, but Kathy, Tom, and Loch, all in the cockpit, are on edge. Even though it's dark they can see each and every black wave just as it hits the boat, and they continually brace themselves for the following impact. Tom tries to reassure Kathy that the *Almeisan* is performing superbly, but he does acknowledge that neither he nor the boat has ever been through anything even remotely like this.

About 3 a.m., Kathy, who has become somewhat accustomed to the roar of the waves, hears something even louder, and turns to port just in time to see a rush of white water avalanching down on the boat. Before the liquid mass strikes, she knows she and her crew-mates are in deep trouble, but there's no time even to shout. The wave charges right through the cockpit, blowing out the curtains and Plexiglas windows, burying the crewmembers under its turbulence and sweeping Kathy out of the boat. The *Almeisan* rolls onto her side, her mast plunging underwater, and continues rolling.

Loch and Tom are hurled toward starboard, arms, legs, elbows, and knees slamming into the side of the cockpit. For a split second Loch wonders what has happened because the roaring sound has ended and it's deadly quiet. Then he realizes he's underwater and knows the boat has capsized. He can feel his harness tugging around his chest, and he knows that is the only reason he's not been carried away by the wave. *Just stay still,* he tells himself; *the boat will come back up.*

In the cabin below, Chris is buried under a torrent of water. He doesn't know which way is up, and feels a rising panic. Then he remembers that as a child he was taught to blow bubbles if he's ever trapped underwater and doesn't know where the surface is. And so he releases air from his mouth, and tries to follow the bubbles, but realizes he's ensnared under a blanket, and furiously tries to claw his way out from under it. He can feel the boat righting itself, and he is able to raise his head above the water. He can't believe what he sees. The large window above the salon is gone. Had he kept his initial position on the bench, his head would have been directly under the window, and he would have been severely injured or even killed by the exploding glass.

Outside, as the boat rights herself, Loch knows that somehow he's still in the cockpit, and yells, "Tom! Tom, are you here?"

"I'm here!" answers Tom, slumped on the cockpit floor.

"Kathy!" shouts Loch. "Kathy, where are you?"

Loch hears Kathy scream, but her voice seems far away, and he can't locate her in the darkness.

Tom hears her too, and frantically shouts, "Kathy, hang on!"

"Help! Help!" Kathy yells.

Loch feels around in the cockpit and finds Kathy's tether, relieved to feel weight on the other end. He follows the line to the starboard aft side, sees Kathy, and shouts for Tom. She is outside the boat, her hands desperately clutching the life line that circles the deck. Her legs are in the water and it's impossible for her to lift them all the way to the deck. The *Almeisan* is still racing down waves, and the sea is tugging at Kathy's legs, loosening her grip.

Loch and Tom each have a hold of one of Kathy's arms. Chris is now on deck and he adds his strength to pulling Kathy back on board.

Ron staggers from his berth, nursing another contusion on his head. When the boat rolled he was thrown down into the overhead, which was below him, and then fell back into his bunk when the boat came back up. He's now wading through a foot and a half of water as he struggles toward the companionway, where he can hear yelling from above. His foot slips off some debris and lands on a sharp object, slicing a deep gash into his flesh. Hobbling up the steps, he sees the other men dragging Kathy into the cockpit, and he knows exactly what happened—and that Kathy is lucky to be alive.

For a second all five sailors are together in the cramped cockpit, trying to catch their breath and process what has happened. The waves are now striking the boat on the starboard side, and the crew realizes that not only did the *Almeisan* capsize but the rogue wave had also pivoted the vessel bow to stern.

Tom recovers from the shock first, heading below, shouting, "We've got to get the engine started!"

The rest of the crew follows the captain down the companionway. Loch is shocked—the cabin looks as if it's been blown apart by a hand grenade. The large starboard side window is now a gaping hole, and even the wood window frame is shattered. Water is still splashing through the opening, and all manner of debris—cans, food, pots, shards of wood, and even some of the floorboards—are sloshing about. He runs to the aft cabin and searches through the mess for PFDs and bug-out bags (plastic pouches for personal items such as wallets and passports). When he locates a few he stumbles back to the salon, noting that the water has risen higher than it was just a minute earlier.

Tom is able to start the engine, but the boat's bilge pump won't work properly as debris keeps clogging it. Then the captain grabs the radio. "Mayday, Mayday, Mayday, this is the sailing vessel *Almeisan.*" Next he grabs the EPIRB and sets it off, before handing it to Chris, saying, "Keep this with you every second!" The EPIRB's light is flashing, and Chris takes the device's nylon strap and wraps it securely around his wrist.

Tom assesses the damage, the rising water, the broken window and companionway hatch, and motions for Loch to follow him back up to the cockpit. Once there, he shouts, "It's time to prepare the life raft! Do you agree?"

Loch hollers back, "Yes, we're taking on water, we've got to get off!"

"Tell the others! Tell them to get ready!" shouts Tom.

Loch half slides, half crawls down the companionway, to where Ron, Chris, and Kathy are talking.

Loch shouts, "We've got to go! We're leaving the boat!"

The crew is stunned. Everything is happening too fast, much too fast.

CHAPTER ELEVEN

THE LIFE RAFT

Abandoning a boat to get into a life raft is perhaps the biggest and most difficult decision a captain can make, and choosing what to do all depends upon each individual situation. On the one hand there is the old rule of thumb, "Never leave a vessel unless you are stepping up into a life raft." This saying drives home the message that your vessel must actually be sinking before you even consider getting off. The problem a captain faces, however, is that sinking doesn't always happen gradually, and death can occur even before the boat is actually on its way to the bottom.

Crewmembers can become trapped inside the boat and never have time to escape. This is especially true on powerboats, where there is no weighted keel to bring the vessel back upright. A capsize on a powerboat means the boat is going to stay upside down, whereas on a sailboat, the vessel should—if its integrity is intact—eventually right itself. Having a sailboat recover after capsizing, however, doesn't ensure that the people on board will still be alive. All sorts of bad things can happen. If you are in the cockpit, your tether can break and you can be swept away. Or the tether holds, but you are unable to get back on the boat and you are dragged to your death. And if you are below in the cabin, you can be killed by the violence of the capsizing, breaking your neck or splitting your skull. A severe knockdown can cause small objects such as a simple can of tuna fish to become a deadly missile, and large objects, such as a microwave or a refrigerator, to catapult from their mountings and crush a person. Even if you avoid those killer injuries, there's no guarantee you will be able to escape alive if a hatch or window breaks. Sailors have become injured in the roll and drowned in the tons of seawater charging inside the vessel.

Tom certainly hates the thought of abandoning his beloved *Almeisan,* but he also knows that Kathy could have been swallowed by the sea if her tether broke, and that Ron and Chris could have been killed in the confines and chaos belowdecks. The captain also realizes the integrity of the *Almeisan* is now compromised, because the five- by two-foot salon window is blown out. Oncoming waves will send more water through the broken window, and if the boat incurs another knockdown, *thousands* of gallons of seawater will come flooding in, and this time the boat may not recover. Tom fears that if they stay on the *Almeisan*—which he believes is taking on more water with each passing second—another rogue wave is going to be catastrophic, and there may not be time to abandon ship. He wants to get off while everyone is still in one piece, still breathing, and while there's time to prepare and launch the raft.

But Ron, also an experienced sailor, doesn't see it this way. He isn't convinced the *Almeisan* is sinking, and he views the vessel as a kind of life raft itself, only bigger and safer than the inflatable one. He feels that it's premature to leave the boat, knowing that doing so is an irrevocable choice and that once they abandon ship they will have used up all their options. The sheer size of the waves has given Ron pause, and he pictures the life raft careening down waves like a roller coaster, bodies flying and crashing into one another. Ron has always thought a sailor should stay with the boat as long as it's afloat, and he wants to make his stand—and stake his survival—on the *Almeisan.*

Loch passes Ron on his way to get survival gear, telling him to be ready to go. Ron answers, "Why? We don't know the boat is sinking."

But Loch has decided that Tom is right, that staying on the boat will likely be a death sentence. Loch says, "Come on, we're going!"

Ron shakes his head in concern. Now, however, is not the time to argue, and he defers to Loch and the captain.

Chris has listened to the exchange, and finds that the last few minutes have a surreal feel to them. So much has happened, so much has changed. He thinks how fragile the boat now feels, how minuscule they all are compared to the raging seas around them. Then a pragmatic thought brushes away his observations, and he looks at the EPIRB in his hand that Tom has asked him to hold. *Wherever the EPIRB goes, that's where I'm going.*

Kathy isn't certain about the best course of action. She agreed with the need to issue the Mayday and activate the EPIRB, but deploying the life raft has its pros and cons, making it difficult to make a snap decision. *One thing's for sure,* she thinks, *I'm going to trust my intuition in the future.* She recalls her earlier decision to ignore her reservations about leaving on a voyage so early in the spring. Kathy is particularly upset at herself for not taking action when she wanted to disembark after rounding Montauk when they heard the warning from the passing sailboat. Now she wonders if she will be alive to see another sunrise.

Kathy doesn't want to go back out on the deck where she almost drowned just fifteen minutes earlier, but feels there is little choice. They are all going to abandon ship. And so she follows the men up the companionway ladder, where Tom is waiting. It's hard to see Tom's face, but she can see his large eyeglasses, and can only imagine the pressure he is under. She notices the hardtop above the cockpit has a large open crack down the middle and its aft starboard support is sticking right through the hardtop, as if a giant fist had pounded down on the covering.

"Tom!" shouts Chris. "Did anyone hear your Mayday?" The wind is blasting and, together with the seas, makes an awful roar. Chris isn't sure Tom has heard him, because Tom first turns on the lights attached to the mizzen spreader and then lurches toward the aft deck, intent on deploying the raft. Chris can now see the white-capped peaks of the menacing waves towering above the boat and he worries about Tom's ability to balance on the pitching and plunging deck. It flashes through his mind that Tom is at the end of his energy reserve, and now susceptible to a heart attack. Chris asks Loch what he can do to help, and Loch says to just hang on a second, while he goes below to bring up two ditch bags filled with survival supplies.

On the aft deck, Tom removes additional ditch bags from their canisters and attaches them to the boat so they won't be washed overboard. The flood lamps hanging on the underside of the mast spreader cast a pale yellow light on Tom, the deck, and the roiling water surrounding it. The boat careens wildly with each passing wave, but somehow the exhausted captain keeps on his feet.

Next, Tom unfastens the life raft from its canister, removes it, and pushes the raft forward toward the cockpit. He quickly ties off the painter from the raft to a stanchion, then shoves the raft over the port side of the boat, where it auto-inflates with its open doorway facing the boat. Immediately the wind fills the orange raft and it is blown away from the boat as if it were a paper bag. The raft's flight is stopped short when it reaches the very end of the twenty-five-foot painter. Tom is holding onto the nylon painter, a flat, extremely thin three-eighths inch of strap that is difficult to grip. He hands the line to Loch, shouting, "I'll get some gloves to help us pull it back! If we don't get it back quick, the painter will break!"

Ron assists Loch, but the line is so thin it cuts the flesh on his fingers and palms, and the two men make little progress. Tom returns with two sets of gloves and now the men are able to get a better hold on the tether and bring the raft to within five feet of the boat, but they cannot get it any closer. Tom goes aft to see if the line is fouled, while Ron and Loch, now assisted by Chris, wrap the line around the port winch to give their hands a rest. The winch handle, however, has been washed overboard, and they have no way to pull it closer.

The raft is too far from the boat to board safely, and with the waves pummeling it, Loch fears the thin tether will break and their sole means of escape will be taken by the seas. He simply cannot let this happen—somehow he's got to get a heavier line secured to the raft. He shouts an idea to Ron, but the wind is too loud for him to be heard.

Loch decides to act, risking all. First he detaches his safety harness tether from the lifeline that rings the boat, and puts one foot outside the lifeline on the gunwale, all the while staring at the opening in the raft's canopy. Then he dives.

Incredibly, he shoots through the raft's doorway, skidding along the raft's bottom on his belly. He rolls to his side, then to his knees, and in the dim orange glow frantically clips his harness tether onto a rope that circles the inside of the raft.

Loch sticks his head out the doorway. "Toss me a line!" he shouts to Ron.

Ron, who had been caught off guard by Loch's dive into the raft, scrambles for a heavy line, and once found, throws it into Loch's outstretched arms. Loch looks for a place to tie off the line, and, seeing none, begins to pull on the line hand over hand, with Ron doing the same on the other end. When the raft is next to the port side of the boat, Loch reaches up and grabs one of the boat's stanchions. Then disaster hits.

An enormous wave slams the *Almeisan* on the starboard side, sending her over on a ninety-degree angle. Torrents of green water sweep over her deck, washing bodies into the sea.

CHAPTER TWELVE

OVERBOARD!

Chris is knocked chest-first onto the deck, breaking his fall at the last second with his arms. Tons of green water wash over him, but he knows he's inside the boat because his hands and knees scrape the wooden deck sliding beneath him. When he recovers and rises into a crouch, he doesn't immediately see anyone else, and for a moment he has the sickening thought that they have all been swept away. Then he notices Kathy still on her feet, hunkered down in the cockpit. He looks aft, and there is no one on the deck. But the glow from the mizzen spreader lights illuminates the ocean's surface behind the boat, and he spots Tom in the water, drifting away in the churning seas. He knows it's Tom because the light reflects off his eyeglasses, even though he is fifty feet behind the *Almeisan*. Chris's first thought is to use the GPS "man overboard" function to pinpoint the location, but he realizes it had already been used when Kathy went overboard earlier, and neither he nor Kathy knows how to reset it. In addition, the GPS chart plotter is inoperable from water damage. Precious seconds tick by.

Chris scrambles on deck to deploy the life slings when he hears a frantic shout from a forward position. He turns toward the sound but can see nothing. Then he spots an arm clutching a stanchion supporting the lifeline cable that encircles the boat.

The arm belongs to Ron Burd, who has been swept off the boat by the rogue wave but somehow maintained a grip on the stanchion. The lower half of his torso is in the water, and he's trying to get one foot up on the gunwale. His feet are facing the bow, his head aft, and his safety tether is stretched taught as water cascades over him. His grip is weakening as the seas pull at him. Ron knows that if he loses his handhold and is dragged alongside the boat, it might be impossible for anyone to help pull him on board.

Chris grabs the top of Ron's safety harness, shouting, "You've got to throw your leg up!"

Ron uses every ounce of energy he has left to twist his waist and kick one leg up, managing to get his foot on the gunwale beneath the lifeline. That gives him just enough leverage to assist Chris, and Chris drags Ron back on board.

Chris turns to look aft for Tom, but only sees huge gray waves and frothing tops.

Kathy and Chris help Ron into the cockpit, where Ron collapses, completely soaked and spent. He feels the chill of the blasting wind, and slides lower for some protection. His whole body begins shaking as his mind processes how close he came to being taken by the sea.

Ron looks around and stammers, "Where's Loch and Tom?"

Chris, exhausted and shivering, has sat down next to him, and lifts his head to meet Ron's gaze. "They're gone. Both swept away. I saw Tom in the water far behind the boat."

Ron is stunned. He thinks of the two men he was just getting to know. *They're either already dead from drowning, and if not, they will be from hypothermia.* Then Ron remembers the life raft.

"What about the life raft?"

"I think I saw it about twenty feet beyond Tom," says Chris.

Kathy looks at Chris and says, "If Loch is still in the raft, maybe he can get Tom."

"God, I hope so," says Ron, teeth chattering. "The life raft is their only chance."

When the big rogue wave sent the *Almeisan* careening on her side, Tom was flung so hard into the sea his safety tether broke the jackline encircling the boat that it was attached to. Loch, who was in the raft, never saw the wave or even heard its roar, but he felt its power as if being hit by a speeding car. He was forced downward several feet and felt a yank on his safety harness, and then no tension at all. In that instant he knew the worst had happened; the line encircling the raft had broken, because when the sea finally released Loch, he came gasping to the surface, completely outside the raft.

Fighting to keep his head above the churning foam, Loch took everything in at once; he saw the wind-driven life raft blown into the darkness, and saw the *Almeisan*—eerie lights still shining on the mizzenmast—careening wildly, seventy feet away, and getting smaller and smaller as the seas put distance between them. There was simply no way he could swim and keep up with the vessel, which made a much larger target for the wind to push.

Now Loch shouts toward the vessel, but has little hope the crew will hear him. A wave of despair envelops him, as he considers how utterly alone he is in the black abyss of raging water.

Suddenly he hears an answering yell, but it's coming from a different direction than the boat. He swims toward the voice, but the colossal walls of water pummel him, driving him several feet down before he kicks to the surface. Loch coughs up seawater, catches his breath, and shouts, "I'm here! I'm here!"

Again he hears the shout and knows it's Tom, also in the water.

The two men claw at the seas, desperately swimming toward each other before they become further separated in the abyss. They are exhausting themselves with the effort, but nothing else matters at this moment.

Suddenly, as Loch emerges on the other side of a wave, he hears Tom shout from nearby, and there he is, no more than five feet away, doing his best to close the gap between them. A wave buries them both, but when they fight to the surface they clutch at each other's safety harness, not wanting to be yanked apart in the coal black night. Each man clips his tether to the other's harness. Approximately ten feet of line is between the two men.

As the waves pummel the men, sometimes they surface side by side, but other times they end up on opposite sides of the wave, and are dunked separately by the next one. The ten feet of tether is jerked violently, wrenching their bodies unexpectedly. They feel like yo-yos on a string, and they pray the tethers will hold.

Each man has a bulky, orange-colored foam life vest strapped over his foul-weather gear, but still the waves drive them downward. They quickly realize that when they come to the surface they must orient themselves and locate the direction of the next oncoming wave so that they can turn their heads away. When they don't, they take a tremendous slap in the face as their heads are whipped backward and water is forced up their nostrils.

Both men search the darkness for the *Almeisan,* and they glimpse the masthead light, and then the spreader lights, now more than two hundred feet away. Then the boat disappears from view, blocked by a thirty-foot wall of water. Both men shout for help. When they get their next glimpse at the vessel's lights, they stare in utter despair, recognizing that the boat is further away, far beyond the sound of their yells.

From his time on watch, Tom knows his boat is drifting at three knots, and he watches the masthead light vanish into the gloom, gone from view for good.

Waves slam the two men every twenty to thirty seconds, and between each assault, when they are in the same trough, they have a few seconds to shout.

"Just hang on!" shouts Loch. "The Coast Guard will have heard our EPIRB!"

Neither man, however, kids himself about help coming anytime soon.

Fighting the seas takes incredible energy, and both men have already spent the prior two days working round the clock with almost no sleep; they are bone tired already. Tom in particular has been under incredible strain, first fretting over the crew's comfort, then their safety, and finally their very lives. Ironically, he might not even have deployed the life raft if he were alone on the boat or if it were just he and Loch on board. Abandoning ship meant the end of the *Almeisan,* and the *Almeisan* was part of his very soul. If it was just his own life in danger, he may have chosen to risk it, and tried to save his boat. But with crew on board, the *Almeisan* had to take a backseat to their safety, and he felt the risk of staying on the damaged boat was greater than in the life raft. And now the very worst possible string of events has happened. Tom knows he might die but he's still worried about the crew, alone on a sinking boat with no life raft. He says a silent prayer for their safety.

Tom turns his attention to his own situation and takes stock of what he has on his body. It's not much: a T-shirt, pants, foul-weather pants and coat, safety harness, and life preserver with a three-inch strobe light attached to it. He's thankful for the strobe and the life preserver, but he can't help but think about one thing he doesn't have—drinking water. Dehydration will set in quickly, particularly with the way the men are expending energy and ingesting seawater. They're already thirsty and craving fresh water.

If they should survive the beating inflicted by the waves, Tom knows hypothermia is the other major concern. The temperature of the ocean is 73 degrees (Fahrenheit), thanks to the Gulf Stream, and while that may sound warm, it's far lower than the body temperature a person needs to maintain for survival. A healthy body temperature is 98.6 degrees, and immersion in water colder than that lowers the body's warmth. This process occurs much more quickly than many people would expect: water sucks away body heat twenty-four times faster than air of the same temperature.

Every individual's tolerance to hypothermia is different, and charts reflect this wide swing, with the U.S. Coast Guard hypothermia chart showing that in 70- to 80-degree water, the time of survival ranges from as little as three hours to "indefinite," with indefinite assuming calm seas. This same chart, however, shows an equally disturbing category, labeled "exhaustion or unconsciousness." In water temperatures between 70 and 80 degrees, a person will succumb to exhaustion or unconsciousness in three to twelve hours. In these unforgiving seas, that's as good as a death sentence because in total exhaustion or unconsciousness neither Loch nor Tom will be able to keep his head above the foaming ocean's surface. Death may be officially attributed to drowning, but the hypothermia will be the genesis.

Other than their life vests, the two men do have a couple of things working in their favor that may buy them an extra hour or two. Their wet foul-weather jackets and pants—in addition to regular pants and T-shirts—will help slow the process of hypothermia by trapping a bit of water warmed by the body close to the skin. Any extra ounce of fat will also help insulate the body, and this is the one time in Tom and Loch's life that being a few pounds overweight will actually protect their health. (Body mass plays an important part in delaying hypothermia, which is why adults usually outlive children trapped in the same chilling situation.) Whenever they can, the two men huddle together for a bit of shared body warmth, although with the seas moving so violently, this warming of the water between them might be marginal at best.

The body itself will fight the cold, by generating heat production through shivering and shaking, but this requires energy, and the men were fatigued even before they hit the water. And of course they are struggling with the waves, expending vigor by the second. Not only must they keep their heads pointed away from each oncoming torrent, they must also claw to the surface after being buried by breaking waves. Instead of conserving energy by just floating, they have no choice but to kick, squirm, and thrash against each avalanching wave—waves that they cannot even see in the dark, but only hear their menacing roar.

Although total exhaustion or unconsciousness may be a few hours away, the men will be feeling the effects of hypothermia much sooner as the body's core temperature drops to 95 degrees. A rigidity of their muscles leading to dexterity problems will make their battle all the more difficult and they might become incoherent or fall into a stupor, which will lead to drowning long before the death stage of hypothermia.

The outlook for survival until morning is fair; the outlook for the next twelve hours is grim.

CHAPTER THIRTEEN

DAWN

The Gulf Stream's current may have been partially responsible for the two unusually large waves that hit the *Almeisan,* as well as the two that clobbered the *At Ease* two days earlier. Some experts now think rogue waves—technically defined as any waves more than twice the height for the average current sea state—are to be expected in the Gulf Stream in stormy weather because of the explosive combination of wind and sea current.

In April of 2005, just one month before the *Almeisan*'s fateful voyage, the cruise liner *Norwegian Dawn* was hit by a seventy-foot high rogue wave during a storm off the coast of North Carolina on its way to New York. The ship, more than six hundred feet long, sustained flooding and many broken windows and had to divert to Charleston, South Carolina, for repairs. Many of the passengers had seen enough of the sea and left the ship, opting to take the train to New York. Some of these same passengers later filed a lawsuit against the cruise line, declaring that the ship should have never been out in stormy weather that they claimed routinely produces rogue waves in the Gulf Stream. The plaintiffs cited research from Susanne Lehner, an associate professor of applied marine physics at the University of Miami. "The *Norwegian Dawn* encountered conditions conducive to rogue waves," asserted Lehner. "If you have waves against currents, you can get very high, singular waves." Norwegian Cruise Line felt differently, of course, answering that "the sea had actually calmed down when the wave seemed to come out of thin air at daybreak. Our captain, who has over twenty years on the job, said he never saw anything like it."

During the storm the captain had reduced speed, altered course, activated the ship's stabilizers, and alerted onshore officials of the vessel's progress every four hours. The cruise company contended there was no way the captain could have predicted that a wave more than double the size of all the thousands that preceded it would form. But the plaintiffs' attorney hoped to prove that such a wave could have reasonably been expected and was not an extraordinary circumstance. (A judge denied class action status covering all passengers, instead determining that each of the plaintiffs needed to prove their damages individually. As of this writing, the cases have not gone to trial. However, the National Transportation Safety Board determined that the ship's captain and crew acted properly during the incident.)

While it's arguable whether such rogue waves can be predicted or expected, recent satellite tracking techniques and images are surprising scientists by illustrating that there are far more rogue waves than was formerly thought, and they are not confined to ocean areas with strong currents. German researcher Wolfgang Rosenthal told *National Geographic* that he thought he'd have difficulty finding rogue waves, "but roughly two ships each week are affected." And in one three-week time frame, satellites tracked ten monster waves. It's uncertain if more rogue waves are forming than in the past or if the technology is simply better for verifying their existence, but even inshore boaters—once thought to be safe from rogue waves—are encountering these giants. Amazingly enough, sometimes they appear when no storms are in the area. Martha's Vineyard commercial fisherman Scott Terry was only three miles out from land when a wave more than triple the size of the swells he was motoring through hit his boat. He told the *Boston Globe,* "I've seen lots of swells and a lot of big waves. I've fished in a lot of tough conditions before. But I've never seen anything like that. It just came out of nowhere." The wave was estimated to be fifteen to twenty feet high and it flipped Terry's twenty-four-foot boat, forcing him and his crew to cling to the overturned vessel before they managed to swim to Norman's Island and safety.

The *Almeisan* has already felt the wrath of rogue waves, and if another one hits, the vessel will likely capsize, flood with water through the large broken window and the missing companionway hatch, and not right itself. But Ron, Kathy, and Chris know that even without another monster wave, the vessel might still sink if water continues to fill up the cabin. They have got to find a way to keep the *Almeisan* afloat and make sure help is on the way.

Ron and Kathy go below and wade into the seawater and debris sloshing about. There are a couple of inches of water in the raised salon area, but beyond the salon at either end of the boat, which are a couple of steps down from the salon, the water is knee deep. Despite the violent motion each time a wave hits, Kathy decides the best thing to do is start bailing, and she picks up a bucket and goes at it. Ron lurches to the radios to see if they are working.

Topside, Chris tries to gather his wits in the cockpit. It's 57 degrees and the wind feels much colder. *The three of us are alone in this unfamiliar boat in a storm that seems to be getting worse. This does not look good.* He notices there's a faint hint of light, and soon he can see the oncoming waves more clearly. It looks as if every fourth or fifth wave is a bit bigger than the others and will absolutely crush the boat. He braces himself and shouts, "Hold on! Hold on!" But the *Almeisan* floats up and over the liquid wall. Chris sees another big one coming, and again thinks they will be buried. "Hang on! We're about to get hit!" Again, the vessel rides up the wave and slews sideways down the back side. Now Chris realizes the boat can handle the thirty-footers, and he can only hope there are no larger waves still out there. He's shaking from the cold and sees there's nothing constructive he can do in the cockpit, so he goes below to help the others.

As Chris climbs down the companionway, he shudders when he sees the gaping hole where the salon window was, remembering how he was sleeping below it, knowing it's sheer luck he wasn't severely injured or killed. Then he hears a humming sound and realizes the engine is running despite being partially underwater. He had assumed it had stopped working when the first rogue wave hit, because the instruments in the cockpit were dead. He remembers Tom saying something about how the engine was rigged so that it could pump water out of the boat.

Wading through the water, he opens the engine compartment door and sees the water being churned by the engine pulleys, and that the level of the water is almost up to the induction manifold opening. He reaches into the water with one arm and blindly gropes for a valve that might turn on the engine pump, then quickly steps back, worried his harness life line will get caught in the pulleys.

Just then a wave slams the boat especially hard, and the comforting sound of the engine stops. Chris races to the engine control panel and hits the starter, but it just makes a clicking noise and the engine stays silent, waterlogged and unresponsive.

"Damn!" he shouts.

Kathy stops bailing and steps toward Chris.

"The engine died for good!" shouts Chris. Then he pauses and hollers, "But maybe the bilge pumps will still work since our main batteries are still going!"

Kathy locates a soggy ship's manual and together they find the section detailing the workings of the emergency manual bilge pump in the galley and a second emergency bilge pump located aft. Chris tries different methods to get them going, but nothing works, and so he set his sights on the much smaller maintenance bilge pump located under the galley sink. After hooking this up to the engine batteries, the pump works and Chris breathes a sigh of relief.

His satisfaction is brief—just a couple of minutes later the pump becomes clogged and shuts down. Chris takes the pump apart, removes the debris, and the unit pumps for another few minutes before getting clogged again. Finally, he tries using a kitchen colander for a strainer, and this allows the system to pump a little longer, but it still clogs frequently. And so he hovers over the pump, listening for any noise indicating blockage, and every three or four minutes takes the pump apart and cleans it out.

Ron has had no luck trying different channels on the single-sideband radio, which can transmit farther than the VHF radio. He's gotten considerable radio experience from making voyages on his own boat, as well as from his days as a radio operator in the marines years ago. He decides to give the radio a rest and he joins Kathy in manually bailing. The process is extremely slow because they need to keep one hand on the walls to prevent themselves from falling as the boat heaves one way and then the other. Sections of the sole boards are missing, and sometimes they step into jagged holes, temporarily getting their ankles pinned and sometimes cut. Occasionally a wave sends them sprawling into the water. Kathy is throwing her pails of water out the broken window, and Ron is dumping his out the companionway, where it can drain through the scuppers in the cockpit. After an hour of this exhausting work they realize they have not made a dent in the water level, probably because an equal amount of water is entering the boat each time a wave strikes.

Ron breaks the silence. "This is futile. No matter how much we bail we'll never get ahead and only exhaust ourselves even more."

No sooner are the words out of his mouth than a large wave slams the boat, throwing Ron completely across the salon and over the table, dropping him in a heap on the settee bench.

Kathy drops her pail and struggles to Ron, asking if he's OK. She notices both his hands are bleeding. She locates the first-aid kit and begins to wrap his torn flesh.

Chris joins them at the table. He asks Ron if he's OK, and Ron nods. Then Chris tries to ease the tension, saying to Ron, "Are you going to sell your boat if we get home? I think I might."

Next, they discuss ways to cover the broken window above them, through which seawater showers them. They rummage around the cabin but can find nothing large enough to seal the opening, and they know that if they use a tarp it will be blown to shreds in minutes.

They sit back down by the table, dejected, bracing themselves to offset the wild motion of the boat. Chris says, "Now what?" No one answers. Their situation is looking bleaker by the minute.

All three sailors know that everything depends on whether or not the EPIRB has functioned properly. They have no way of knowing, and all they can do is wait.

CHAPTER FOURTEEN

THE COAST GUARD

Earlier that Sunday morning, hundreds of miles to the northwest of the *Almeisan,* the EPIRB's signal was picked up by the Coast Guard in Boston (District 1) when it was first set off. Unfortunately, the signal had come in without a position. Information contained in the beacon's identification data, however, gave the Coast Guard the name of the vessel, its home port, and phone numbers to contact in the event of an emergency. Coast Guard Boston immediately called those phone numbers and were able to reach logistician Donna Christman, who said she had last spoken to captain Tom Tighe via radio the preceding night at 8 p.m. Donna explained that the EPIRB must surely be an emergency because the captain said they were in stormy seas that were twenty feet and their position was 36°59'N, 67°33'W. She also gave as much information as possible about the vessel, the people on board, the captain's experience, and the safety equipment.

The last known location of the *Almeisan* and its estimated drift rate placed it 465 nautical miles northeast of Coast Guard Station Elizabeth City, North Carolina. This put the vessel outside of District 1's jurisdiction and closer to the resources of District 5, whose Search and Rescue Command center in Portsmouth, Virginia, immediately took over the case. One of the first steps Norfolk took was to activate the AMVER (Automated Mutual-Assistance Vessel Rescue) system, which allowed them to locate ships registered with the system that were closest to the vessel in distress.

Sponsored by the Coast Guard, AMVER is a computer-based and voluntary global ship reporting system that allows rescue coordinators to divert the best-suited ship or ships to the area of distress. Its degree of success is tied directly to the number of merchant vessels in the program and how frequently they report their position.

Originally started in 1958, the genesis of the AMVER concept goes back to the 1912 *Titanic* disaster, when it became clear that as soon as technology allowed, a communication system and procedures needed to be established for the Coast Guard to locate and contact all ships near the distress area. In the case of the *Titanic,* another vessel, the *Californian,* was only ten miles away, but its crew had no idea the doomed passenger liner was sinking because the *Californian*'s sole telegraph operator had closed down the radio for the night. Flares shot from the *Titanic* were seen by people on the *Californian,* but the ship's captain thought they were part of the *Titanic*'s maiden-voyage celebration!

Today, with advanced radio, GPS, and computers, AMVER tracks more than 100,000 voyages annually and has been credited with saving more than 2,000 lives in the last fifteen years. The program has been so successful, particularly in remote sections of the ocean, that it is used by rescue personnel around the world as the quickest way to get help to vessels in distress.

Now, in the first minutes after receiving the *Almeisan*'s EPIRB, the Coast Guard used AMVER to identify a total of four ships within 150 nautical miles of the *Almeisan,* and all were diverted to the distress area. Still, in these stormy conditions, the nearest vessel was at least four hours away. As soon as dawn broke, a ninety-seven-foot-long Coast Guard search plane, a Hercules C-130, was also dispatched from U.S. Coast Guard Air Station Elizabeth City to go to the estimated emergency spot. Once the C-130 gets on scene it will be the eyes and ears for the rescue center and hopefully will establish direct communication with the *Almeisan.*

Helicopter pilot Lieutenant Commander Eric Bader expects a quiet day at his desk as he walks into Coast Guard Air Station Elizabeth City at 7 a.m. Today will be his last day of duty at the station before leaving for graduate school to study aeronautical engineering. He is looking forward to saying good-bye to friends, packing up his belongings, and then heading home to help his wife and two young children organize their household possessions for the movers who are coming the next day.

Tall and lanky, with blue eyes and thinning light brown hair, Bader is known for his sense of humor and laid-back style. Men who have flown missions with him, however, know that in serious situations he can also be a no-nonsense, take-charge type of guy. Fellow Coasties appreciate that mix of the characteristics, and he will be missed at the station.

Originally from Medina, Ohio, and Wichita, Kansas, Bader has served in the Coast Guard for twelve years, starting his career at the Coast Guard Academy. Upon graduation, his first tour of duty—as for virtually every graduate—was aboard a cutter. After serving eighteen months on the *Tahoma,* Bader set his sights on the ultracompetitive flight school, having been influenced by the movie *Top Gun.* Flight school was a grueling eighteen months served in Pensacola, Florida. Upon completing his flight training he served as a helicopter pilot in Astoria, Oregon, before being transferred to Elizabeth City.

Bader still has his morning cup of coffee in his hand when one of his comrades at the station yells out, "Bader, don't get comfortable, looks like we have a SAR [Search and Rescue case] for you."

After being briefed on what little is known about the *Almeisan,* Bader spends the next couple of hours waiting for further orders. As soon as the C-130 arrives at the distress scene, a decision will be made whether or not a helicopter is needed. There's one thing for certain, however; the emergency scene—465 nautical miles northeast of the air station—is way beyond the fuel limit of the HH-60 Jayhawk. Portsmouth Search and Rescue is trying to solve this problem and is in communication with the U.S. Navy vessel *Trenton,* which is out at sea a few miles east of the halfway point between Elizabeth City and the *Almeisan.* The *Trenton* has a landing pad on its deck to accommodate a helicopter, so it's possible Bader's chopper could refuel there. Even with the landing or "lily-padding" on and off the ship, the fuel situation would be at the upper limits of safety boundaries.

Bader knows that not all EPIRB signals are true emergencies, and most EPIRBs get set off accidentally. But he's got a strong feeling that this one is the real thing, and he calls his wife and tells her he may not be home to help with the packing.

If Bader is told to launch, he knows who his crew will be. Audie

Andry will be his copilot. Andry has been in the Coast Guard only two years, but prior to that the good-natured, wholesome-looking thirty-two-year-old has had twelve years of helicopter experience in the U.S. Army as both a mechanic and pilot. His transition into the Coast Guard has been an easy one, and Bader has flown several missions with Andry and knows him to be unflappable.

The flight mechanic working with Andry and Bader on this mission will be James Geramita, a quiet man of thirty-five with a short, stocky build who has seen duty in Savannah, Georgia; Sitka, Alaska; and now Elizabeth City. Among Geramita's duties on board the flight will be hoist operation of the cable used to lift those in distress from the boat or the water via rescue basket or harness.

Rescue swimmer Arthur "A.J." Thompson is the fourth and final member of the team. The 200-pound, six-foot-two swimmer has brown hair with little gray showing through. As far as rescue swimmers go he is considered an "old man" at age thirty-nine, but year after year he is able to pass the rigorous physical testing a swimmer must endure, and he keeps his position as the senior rescue swimmer at Elizabeth City. Like the other three crewmembers, A.J. grew up in the Midwest. When he was nineteen years old, he was looking to leave his hometown of Norwalk, Ohio, and a probable factory job, and thought the Navy would be his way out. After three years as a hospital corpsman in the Navy, A.J. joined the Coast Guard and spent his first year and a half on a cutter. With his medical background he thought becoming a rescue swimmer would be a good fit and a great way to stay in shape. He was admitted into the demanding Aviation Survival Technician/Rescue Swimmer training program, which is designed to first weed out those who can't handle the physical and mental demands of the job. Two of the more grueling aspects of the training are the 800-meter buddy swim, where you drag another person through the water, and a session called the "bullpen." The bullpen involves six instructors who encircle the trainee in the deep end of the pool and act the way a panicked survivor might. One at a time, the instructors basically attack the trainee—clutching, clawing, spinning, and even yanking the rookie to the bottom of the pool. The trainee must use "lifesaving skills" to break the instructors' grip. If the skills are not applied properly, the instructor keeps the trainee in his grip, shouting and thrashing the whole time. As soon as the trainee frees himself properly from one instructor, the next one starts in. It's a brutal test of endurance, but one that just might save the life of a rescue swimmer in a real distress situation.

When A.J. completed and graduated from the several-month-long program, which also included Emergency Medical Technician study, he was assigned to Corpus Christi, Texas, for four years, then on to Kodiak and Sitka, Alaska, for a few more years before being sent to Elizabeth City in 2000. In those twenty years of service, he had practiced being lowered and dropped from helicopters in all kinds of sea conditions, and all kinds of weather, but he had never actually made a life-and-death rescue. He wondered if he'd be one of the only rescue swimmers to retire without having put his training to the test.

Now, A.J. looks out the window of the air station and sees a Jayhawk helicopter being prepared. The Jayhawk weighs 15,500 pounds and can reach speeds of 180 knots, and it uses lots of fuel. It is equipped with two main fuel tanks and two auxiliary tanks. But A.J. notices the tarmac mechanics attaching an additional fifth tank, and he thinks, *If we do launch, it's going to be one long day.*

CHAPTER FIFTEEN

SPECKS IN AN ENDLESS OCEAN

Every wave is a struggle, every breath a fight. Avalanches of water crash down on Loch and Tom, smothering them, pushing their bodies into contorted positions. Each time a wave shoves them under they close their mouths, often tumbling, wondering if they will come back up before they simply cannot hold their breath any longer. Already they have both ingested considerable seawater, and when the men surface in the foam they are coughing, gagging, and vomiting. Then another unrelenting wave bears down on them, repeating the torture.

In the relative quiet of a trough, Loch yells, "Just another half hour until dawn. We've just got to keep going a little longer." He's trying to set a goal, an achievable goal, even though he knows they're going to have to stay afloat well past daylight.

A wave dunks them both before Tom shouts back, "Are you cold yet? I'm shivering, but it's too early for hypothermia."

Loch responds, "I don't feel cold but I'm shaking. Must be from shock."

Just a few minutes later, both men stop shivering, grateful that the hypothermia is at bay for now. In the east a smudge of dim light develops, and slowly spreads out across the horizon. It allows the men to see the waves more clearly; gray streaked mountains of water, about thirty feet in height. Some waves keep their form and do not break, while others are steeper and collapse upon themselves, and a few advance like surf at a beach, curling and then crashing directly on the men. And every now and then one roars in, much larger than the rest; a snarling, menacing mountain of water forty feet in height.

The irony of their situation is not lost on Tom. At his seminars he stressed safety first, especially at night, explaining that if you get swept overboard in the dark, chances are you will never be found. So he insisted that at night, anyone topside must wear a safety harness and keep its tether clipped to the boat, even during calm weather. Yet despite this precaution his own tether had snapped the thick wire lifeline encircling the sailboat.

Tom turns to Loch, shaking his head, saying, "Isn't this the way I said it would be like if someone went overboard at night?"

Loch can only nod. He knows the monumental dilemma they are in, knows the boat—with the EPIRB—has drifted far away, and knows they are expending significant energy on each and every wave. They can't just float, because the wave action, probably coupled with their life vests, works to turn their feet toward the oncoming wave trains, which means they would be facing the seas. So they have to use their arms to paddle and their legs to kick to hold position so their backs will be to the waves.

Every now and then they take a quick look back and see a wave cresting high above before breaking on them like a rock slide. When they finally come to the surface they have learned not to breathe right away and instead wait for several inches of foam to slide past.

Loch decides to try not to look at the oncoming waves; it's just too terrifying. Instead he attempts to judge by their sound when they will strike. He puts up the hood of his foul-weather jacket and notices how it helps channel the water around his head as it rushes by. He encourages Tom to do the same. Tom has trouble reaching back to free his hood, and Loch moves closer to help him. Together they get the hood in place and then try to develop a rhythm of anticipating each hit and maintaining position with their heads pointed away from the seas.

They are glad for the bit of light that dawn has brought, but now that they can see the storm-tossed seas more clearly, the hopelessness of their situation weighs heavily on their spirits. Even if rescue comes later in the day, they know they are mere specks in the endless ocean, and anyone on a ship or in an aircraft will find it next to impossible to spot a bobbing head in the churning waves.

Around 7 a.m., the constant exertion is making it difficult for

Tom to continue holding position. A wave hits him head-on, sending him spinning backward as if punched by a fist.

Loch swims up tight to Tom and offers words of encouragement, helping him face away from the next advancing wave. Tom answers that he's OK, but his voice is now labored and rasping.

The two men try to stay just a couple of feet apart, and they talk about how long it will be before the Coast Guard is on scene looking for them. Tom thinks that given the distance they are from shore, coupled with the weather conditions, it will take aircraft at least another hour or two before they are in the area. This gives the men a new goal to shoot for: endure two more hours and hope for a plane or even a ship.

Because they are on the eastern side of the Gulf Stream, in an area known as the Sargasso Sea, a fair amount of seaweed is floating about. Loch grabs a strip of seaweed and stuffs it into one of his foul-weather pockets.

Tom watches, and with a bemused look says, "What are you doing?"

"Gathering food," replies Loch. "If we're going to be here awhile we're going to need to eat."

Tom smiles and shakes his head.

Loch marvels that despite Tom's weakening condition, he can still smile. Loch has read about people in similar situations, how some simply give up and how others sob and curse their bad luck. And yet here's Tom, uncomplaining, even showing a flash of humor, doing his best despite the long odds. It gives Loch a shot of courage, a bit of inspiration, and he thinks, *If Tom can cope and stay calm, I can too.*

Just after 9 a.m. the solid overcast of clouds breaks up a bit, and through the opening, a shaft of golden sunlight shines through. The ray of light angles down to the ocean from the east and illuminates a small patch of the sea not far from the men. When a wave passes through the beam of light it turns from menacing gray to shimmering gold. Both Loch and Tom are in awe of this beauty in the chaos around them. Neither man has ever seen anything like it and they stare at the ocean's surface, mesmerized by the hues of green, gray, tan, and gold that play on the waves.

Soon the clouds reconverge, blotting out the sun. Tom and Loch get back to the business of enduring each wave, surviving the next few minutes.

Tom is having a hard time keeping his hood up, and when a bigger wave hits, it knocks the breath right out of him. He surfaces in the wrong position, and the next comber sweeps directly into his face, engulfing him in the turbulence before he finally recovers. He coughs and spits up water, trying to clear his airways.

Loch swims to Tom and tries to help turn him in the right direction, but another wave looms above them, crashing down, separating the men. Loch catches his breath in the trough and tries again to assist Tom, but the next wave spins them, burying them in the wild white froth. It's useless, and Loch knows it. There's nothing he can do for Tom until the seas subside, and in Loch's estimation, the wind and waves have not eased but instead seem to be worsening.

CHAPTER SIXTEEN

WORDS FROM THE HEAVENS

Considering that Ron, Kathy, and Chris met just six days earlier, they mesh quite well under incredible pressure. They have to. Their very survival depends on it, and they go out of their way to be outwardly positive and keep their fears to themselves. After an hour of nonstop bailing they are wedged around the salon table, catching their breath, not saying much. Their instincts for survival have forged them into a team of sorts, but there is no one person in charge, no individual delegating duties or influencing decisions. Maybe that's why they feel close, feel that they can get through this with a little luck and each person doing his best. But so far their best hasn't been quite good enough; the boat continues its wild ride, listing to starboard with water sloshing throughout. The free water in the cabin makes each roll more pronounced and recovery longer. More water enters through the broken window and companionway when larger waves wash over the deck.

They begin devising a plan for abandoning ship. They discuss tethering themselves together and taking as many of the emergency provision canisters as possible, including the medical supply canister and flare canister. If they have to leave the vessel, Chris will be the one to grab the EPIRB and secure it in the pocket of his foul-weather jacket. The thought of going into the water without a life raft is terrifying, but now is the time to plan, not when more disaster strikes.

Nerves are raw. Ron and Kathy are still reeling from being tossed out of the boat just a couple of hours earlier, and they have no desire to go topside. Chris decides to take a quick look and climbs into the cockpit, where the roar of the wind is deafening. He sees that the storm has not eased one bit but continues to rage, clawing at the boat

88

as if looking for a new weakness to exploit. He scans the horizon for a possible rescue ship, but with the towering waves, the flying spume and spray, and the pouring rain, it's difficult even to tell where the ocean ends and the sky begins. It's not only dangerous but cold in the cockpit, and Chris scurries back down the companionway ladder to the shelter of the cabin.

Chris sees that Kathy has tied loops in a long line, thinking that they can tie themselves together if the boat starts to go down and they have time to jump off. Ron is back on the radio. Chris can hear Ron saying, "Mayday, Mayday, Mayday, this is the sailing vessel *Almeisan*." Over and over Ron repeats the message, trying different frequencies. Chris goes to Ron and asks if his voice is getting tired, offering to take over sending out the distress message. It's approximately 9:15 a.m.

Suddenly both men stop talking. A faint voice is on the radio. "Sailing vessel *Almeisan*, this is the Coast Guard aircraft 1503. We are heading toward your position. We will have better radio communication shortly. The motor vessel *Sakura Express* is also coming to your aid. Tell us your emergency."

To Ron Burd those words could have been from heaven itself. For a second he is overcome with emotion, and he steadies himself to reply.

Chris hollers to Kathy, "Kathy, we've got the Coast Guard!"

Now all three sailors are crowding around the radio. Ron relays how two crewmembers were swept overboard while readying the life raft, and three crewmembers are on board the *Almeisan*, which is damaged. Then he adds, "We have taken on lots of water and we're bailing. We all have our PFDs on and everyone on board is OK."

The pilots on the aircraft, a C-130 fixed-wing airplane, can barely hear Ron, but they now know just how serious the situation is. However, the part of Ron's briefing that mentioned the life raft is misunderstood, and when the pilots radio Portsmouth Coast Guard they say two people went into a life raft that broke free of the vessel and three people remain on board. In Portsmouth, the radio operator alerts all involved rescue personnel that the C-130 has communication with the *Almeisan* and that "two persons on board abandoned ship into life raft."

This mix-up in communications has grave consequences. The Coast Guard will now search for both the life raft and the *Almeisan,* but not for anyone in the water.

Now the pilots need to pinpoint the *Almeisan's* position. They ask Ron to do a slow count from one to five and back again, hoping they can use their radio direction finder to get a fix on the sailboat.

Several minutes go by, and the pilot then announces, "OK, *Almeisan,* we have your position. We will be there shortly. When we get on scene we will drop a life raft."

The spirits of the three sailors soar. The Coast Guard knows where they are; the EPIRB's signal was heard after all. They start talking about what they will do with the life raft, wondering if the Coast Guard will have them keep it aboard the *Almeisan* for backup after they retrieve it or if they will want them to immediately evacuate. But first they have to secure the life raft package, which will not be easy in fifty-knot winds.

At approximately 9:45 a.m., the roar of a plane is heard above the crashing waves. Kathy and Chris climb to the cockpit and see the most welcome sight of their lives: the white and red C-130, buffeted by the wind, is making a slow, high circle of their crippled boat.

Below, Ron listens carefully as the pilot explains that the *Sakura Express* is the closest vessel to the *Almeisan,* but it is still at least two hours away. The pilot also explains that the *Almeisan's* location is beyond the fuel capacity of helicopters from either Bermuda or the United States, but efforts are under way to have a helicopter from Elizabeth City fly partway out and refuel on a Navy ship. The pilot finishes the message with this instruction: "We are going to drop you a floating package with a life raft. Someone is going to have to be on deck with a boat hook to pull it in from the sea."

Chris and Kathy climb into the cockpit, clip their safety harnesses to pad-eyes, and with a boat hook ready, wait to perform the retrieval. They know it won't be easy, especially as the *Almeisan* crests a wave top, teetering for a second, where they feel most vulnerable to the full fury of the wind. As the boat careens down the back of the wave, Chris can't help think that one misstep while trying to retrieve the raft could mean the end. He tells himself, *What-*

ever you do, don't go overboard now, you've come too far. We've had enough bad luck with life rafts.

The C-130 comes thundering out of the clouds, flying low and directly toward the boat. When the plane is above the *Almeisan*, Chris and Kathy see a package drop from the aircraft, but before it even reaches the ocean the wind hurls it out of sight. A wave hits the *Almeisan* like concrete, knocking the two sailors to the deck.

The C-130 makes a wide turn and within a few minutes is making another pass at the boat. Ron shouts up to Chris and Kathy that they are going to come in lower and this time drop a dewatering pump.

This time the package lands close to the *Almeisan*, but with the vessel drifting faster than the package, it's lost within the seas in just two seconds.

Precious minutes go by, and again the C-130 makes a low pass and drops another pump package. It lands just a few feet from the boat, but before Chris can reach out with the boat hook it is far behind the drifting boat.

Drenched and frustrated, Chris and Kathy go back below and wade through the wreckage to join Ron by the radio. They can hear the C-130 pilot talking to the *Sakura Express*, as he tells the ship's captain that they have located the *Almeisan*'s life raft at position 37°20.7'N, 66°57.5'W. The Coast Guard pilot tells the ship to go to the life raft before heading to the *Almeisan*.

Back in Portsmouth, the radio operator announces: "POB [persons on board] life raft are the captain and first mate. The 1503 [C-13] has not established communications with life raft. The USNS *Seay* determined they are 150 nautical miles to the NW of life raft position. Made decision to divert even though they don't have a helo on board."

A minute later, Portsmouth makes a request to Elizabeth City Air Station: "We would like to preposition the 60 [helicopter] on the USNS *Trenton* to sit, refuel, and wait to see if the AMVER vessels are able to assist and how the situation plays out."

There is more discussion, however, about how the sea conditions are so rough that they are beyond the safety parameters of a helicopter landing on a ship. In addition, the C-130 is near their "bingo" fuel limit; when they hit the bingo point, they will have just enough fuel remaining to make it back to base safely, with absolutely no extra fuel should something go wrong. Senior Coast Guard officials decide the situation is serious enough that if needed they will waive the helicopter's safety restrictions for landing on a vessel, and they will also allow the C-130 to remain on scene right up to "bingo."

Portsmouth then adds: "Three POB are in good health and spirits. They were not able to get the raft or the pumps dropped but are doing fine waiting until help arrives."

Of course Ron, Chris, and Kathy cannot hear Portsmouth, but the C-130 pilot explains that their fuel is low, and will soon have to turn back. They say another C-130 is being prepared to launch.

The three sailors huddle by the radio waiting for more instructions. Several minutes go by before Ron tries to raise the pilot, with no luck. That's when he notices that the light on the radio is out.

The main battery banks have gone dead.

CHAPTER SEVENTEEN

"NO PERSONS ON BOARD"

Jayhawk helicopter copilot Audie Andry does not let the blue skies and gentle breeze at Air Station Elizabeth City fool him. He knows from listening to the C-130 pilot reports that the distress scene is going to be a nightmare, with slashing rain and fifty-knot winds. He and his fellow flight crewmembers—commander Bader, mechanic Geramita, and rescue swimmer A. J. Thompson—could be facing a grueling fifteen- or sixteen-hour rescue event.

SAR coordinators have decided to have the Jayhawk pre-position and refuel aboard the Navy ship *Trenton*, in case the AMVER vessels cannot perform the rescues. Having a Jayhawk refuel on a Navy ship is certainly not routine, but Andry thinks that the way this day is shaping up, nothing will be normal. The little bit he's heard about the *Almeisan* doesn't even make sense: that the captain and the first mate are likely in a life raft and that three other people are on board the sailboat. Andry decides this version of the events—which implies the captain and first mate had willingly abandoned ship without the others—is simply too strange to be entirely correct, and there must be more to the story.

As they board the aircraft, the four-man flight crew are dressed in dry exposure suits and each has a helmet with communication equipment in it so they can converse over the roar of the spinning rotors. As aircraft commander, Eric Bader has his choice of the left or right seat, and he decides to take the right seat so that if they have a hoist operation he can get a visual on the cable, because it too is located on the right side of the chopper. Otherwise, the controls on the left and right side of the cockpit are the same for both Andry and Bader. James Geramita sits behind the pilots in the cabin on the right side next to the door and hoist, while A.J. is in a seat opposite him.

The *Trenton* is 170 miles away from Elizabeth City, and the one-and-a-half-hour flight there is uneventful. Landing on the *Trenton*, however, takes the full concentration of the two pilots. Although the storm is centered another 250 miles east of the Navy ship, it has created eight-foot swells, causing the *Trenton* to pitch and roll. Luckily, the wind is moderate and the pilots have full daylight for the landing, and they accomplish it without incident.

Audie Andry's problems are just beginning, however. Just minutes after they land he begins to feel queasy. The copilot, who is used to being buffeted about by the wind while airborne, feels a different, unfamiliar sensation on board ship, and is soon seasick. He's anxious to get off the rolling vessel and back in the sky. But that's not an option. Even after refueling the helicopter, the *Almeisan* is still too far away, and the sailboat is drifting quite quickly to the east, in the opposite direction of the *Trenton*. The pilots and SAR coordinators know that the helicopter must have enough fuel not only to make it to the *Almeisan*, but also to return later to a land-based landing site. They cannot risk landing on the *Trenton* after the rescue because it will be nighttime and the seas are forecast to be even higher. And so they take their only course of action: have the *Trenton* steam closer to the *Almeisan*.

Andry takes up position on the deck, trying to keep focused on the horizon as waves of nausea pass over him. With each passing mile, the *Trenton* is getting closer to the storm itself, and the seas grow, making the copilot feel even worse. The rest of the three crewmen are fine—even grabbing a bite to eat with the *Trenton* crew—but they make a point to take up positions amidships, where there's the least amount of rolling.

The sailors on board the *Trenton* explain that this will be the second time in two days they will be involved in a rescue. Early Saturday morning the ship received a Mayday from a sailboat called the *Cosmos,* caught in the same storm that was pounding the *Almeisan.*

On board the forty-three-foot sailboat were fifty-six-year-old Captain Ted Weber, and an eighty-three-year-old crewmate, Joseph Wilson. Weber was an experienced sailor with thirty-five years of offshore passages under his belt, but Wilson was on his very first blue-water voyage. The boat was located approximately 250 miles east of the New Jersey coast, and was being battered by waves of thirty and forty feet and winds up to sixty knots.

Weber was taking down a trysail when an enormous wave blind-sided the skipper, sending him sprawling across the deck, then over the boom, one foot becoming entangled in the lazyjacks. The boat heeled on its side, tangling Weber in the rigging, then pitching him into the water. When the *Cosmos* recovered, Weber was hanging upside down above the deck, swinging from the rigging. Remarkably, he managed to free himself and finished getting the sail down.

When he went down the companionway into the cabin, the first thing he saw was blood, lots of blood. Then he heard a moan. Joe Wilson was lying on the sole boards with a six-inch gash in the back of his head.

Weber clutched Joe's head, trying to staunch the flow of blood, but the wound was too deep. When the older man did not respond to Weber's questioning, the captain used his cell phone and called his wife, Cheryl, a nurse practitioner. She asked several questions about Wilson's condition, and they both decided they had better call the Coast Guard.

Ted Weber hailed the Coast Guard on Channel 16, explaining that Wilson was seriously injured. The *Cosmos* was so far offshore that a Coast Guard helicopter would not have enough fuel to reach the scene, nor could it refuel aboard the *Trenton*—which was in the vicinity of the sailboat—because the seas were so violent. Therefore the Coast Guard asked the *Trenton* to steam to the distress scene and try to rescue the injured sailor. Navy officers aboard the *Trenton* realized that the weather conditions were deteriorating by the minute, and they decided to take the unusual step—forced by necessity—to act like the Coast Guard and launch one of their helicopters to remove the injured man while they could still fly. Arriving on scene, the chopper lowered its rescue swimmer, Lee Lyons, into the tempest, and Lyons fought the seas in his mask and fins, reaching the boat on his second attempt. Weber helped pull him on board, and together they brought Wilson up on deck. They put two life jackets on the injured man, and Lyons harnessed himself and Wilson together, clipped them both to the helicopter's hoist cable, and up they went to safety. (When Joe Wilson arrived at a hospital he was found to have fractured several vertebrae in his neck and had a hematoma pressing on his brain, causing him to spend two months in the hospital.) Weber, alone aboard the *Cosmos,* managed to sail the boat west to Atlantic City.

The story of the *Cosmos* gives A.J. an inkling of how bad the conditions will be closer to the storm's center if he and the crew are ordered to go. He hopes he can do as well as the Navy rescue swimmer, but he also knows the *Almeisan* rescue will involve more people than the *Cosmos*: three people on board the damaged vessel, and two more apparently adrift in a life raft. Also, it's getting closer to nightfall, and that's what really worries him. A daytime rescue will be difficult at best, but a night rescue multiplies the perils tenfold. But there's not a damn thing he can do to speed the process; the *Trenton* is steaming as fast as it can.

It's midmorning, and Tom and Loch have been in the ocean several hours, their strength being sapped by each wave that washes over them. Suddenly, both men look to the west. Under the cloud cover, at least a mile distant, a large plane is making a slow circle. The plane completes its loop and makes another one, this time a little closer to the two men. Then it flies directly at them. Loch rips the yellow bug-out bag from his neck and waves it back and forth for all he is worth. Tom does the same.

Before the plane reaches the men, it banks and starts to ascend into the clouds, quickly disappearing from view. The two men are devastated. The plane was less than a quarter mile away before it flew off—so close that they could see its orange stripe, indicating it was a Coast Guard plane. The men don't know it, but this is the same C-130 that was in communication with the survivors on the *Almeisan,* and the flight crew is trying to locate the life raft that they think holds Tom and Loch.

Loch kicks his way close to Tom, who is clearly having difficulty expelling water from his throat and lungs. His breaths come out wheezing, but he gives his friend a weak smile.

96

Loch needs to give words of encouragement—as much for himself as for Tom. "That was a Coast Guard plane! The EPIRB worked. They know we're out here."

Seconds later they hear the plane again, and there it is, off to the left, a mile away. Like before, the plane makes a couple of slow circles, and then breaks off the circling pattern and heads toward the men, who are both waving frantically.

"They see us!" shout Loch. "They're coming right at us!"

Then, just before the plane reaches the men, it banks to the left and rises into the clouds.

Above the crashing of the waves the two men listen to the plane's engine get fainter and within seconds all they can hear is the enraged sound of the sea swirling around them.

No words pass between the men. They both know that the crew on the Coast Guard plane saw nothing but windswept gray seas below them.

Portsmouth Search and Rescue Center has ordered a second C-130 to relieve the first, which must fly back to base because its fuel is running low. When the second C-130 is at the distress scene, it radios back to Norfolk with what the flight crew thinks is good news: they have spotted a life raft. A few minutes later they radio Portsmouth again with this message: "We currently have no communication with the sailing vessel. We have marked the position of the life raft. The *Sakura Express* is two nautical miles away and are asking what kind of tasking you or I would like them to do."

Portsmouth responds: "Roger, have the *Sakura Express* effect any type of rescue they can with the life raft. Are you able to drop another radio to the sailing vessel?"

The pilot of the C-130 answers that they have dropped two pumps and one radio "with no joy." Just as before, the packages are swept away by the colossal seas before the *Almeisan* crew can gather them in.

The 590-foot long Panamanian tanker, the *Sakura Express,* is the closest ship to both the *Almeisan* and the life raft, and because it is part of the AMVER program, it immediately diverts to the distress scene as requested. The tanker, which is hauling jet fuel from St.

Croix to Boston, has a crew of twenty-one, and the seamen are mostly Filipino, the officers Croatian and Filipino.

Having been given the exact position of the life raft from the C-130, it doesn't take the crew of the *Sakura Express* long to spot the orange raft bobbing in the gray seas. A cheer goes up from the men, as they anticipate saving the lives of two survivors thought to be in the raft.

Yet, as the vessel moves in close, oddly, there is no one poking out the door of the life raft and waving. The men on board the tanker wonder if the survivors are injured or perhaps debilitated by hypothermia. Positioning themselves to drift down, a crewman on board the tanker is able to use a grappling hook to snag the life raft. There is still no sign of life from within. The raft's canopy is mostly flattened, and it's hard to tell if anyone is inside. The crew starts hauling the raft up.

A few seconds later the captain of the *Sakura Express* radios the C-130, and the pilot of the C-130 relays the message to Norfolk: "*Sakura Express* is on scene. Picked up the life raft with no persons on board."

For the first time, all rescue personnel realized that Loch and Tom are not in the life raft but instead are alone in the storm-tossed seas. And no one—not the *Sakura Express* crew, not the C-130 crew, not Portsmouth SAR—knows where they are or if they are still alive.

CHAPTER EIGHTEEN

ALONE

Kathy stares at the silent VHF radio. Being able to listen to the Coast Guard and respond to their requests was incredibly comforting, and now she feels more alone than ever.

The C-130 has flown off to search for Loch and Tom, but without radio communication, Kathy, Ron, and Chris aren't sure what's happening. Waves continue to batter the boat, occasionally knocking it far to starboard, sending the crew flying into the wall, floorboards, or equipment. Battered, bruised, and exhausted, the trio can't help but think they have made it this far only to have the *Almeisan* suddenly go down, taking them with it. For the first time their positive, "can-do" attitude wavers, replaced by a palpable anxiety that shows on their weary faces.

Ron breaks the sense of gloom. "Well, they know where we are, so we just have to hang on a little longer."

"Right," says Chris, "let's see what we can do about this radio."

"And we've got to keep bailing," says Kathy. "A lot more water has come in during the last hour."

Kathy notices the single-sideband (SSB) radio has power and is turned on. None of the crew is familiar with this type of radio, but they locate the owner's manual and send out a Mayday on the emergency frequency. When no one answers, the crew figures they are not operating the radio properly. Knowing the SSB is receiving power, Chris tries rewiring the VHF radio to the same circuit breaker as the SSB, but the VHF will still not power up. He is aware that there are two eighty-pound batteries in the forward berth used to power the anchor windlass, but he feels that the motion in the bow, coupled with the debris sloshing about in the knee-deep water, makes retrieving such a heavy object a recipe for injury. Instead, Chris starts disassembling a large rechargeable flashlight in hopes of hardwiring the battery straight to the VHF radio.

Kathy is searching the boat for a handheld VHF radio, but instead finds a battery box under the cabin's aft berth. Inside is a group 24 battery, and she hollers to Chris to let him know of her find.

Meanwhile, Ron hears a C-130 overhead and climbs into the cockpit, waving to let the pilots know they are still on board. The plane circles the boat then flies off again. Ron heads back below to help with the radio repairs.

Chris has given up on the flashlight idea and disconnects the battery Kathy has found in the forward berth before carrying it into the salon, where the VHF radio is located. All three mariners set about securing the battery in a spot beneath the electric distribution panel.

Next, Chris scavenges some duplex wire from the refrigerator compressor and hardwires the VHF radio to the battery, using zip ties to secure the wiring. It is now 2:30 p.m.

"Well," says Chris, "let's hope this works. I'm all out of ideas." The eyes of the three sailors are all on the radio's display panel, as Ron flips the power switch.

A light comes on, and relief sweeps over the trio.

Ron picks up the mike. "This is the *Almeisan*. Can you hear us?"

"Roger," answers the C-130 pilot. "Situation please?"

"Our radio had died but we've got it rigged to a refrigerator battery now. So we are not sure how long we will have it in service. Situation on the boat is the same. We are doing OK, but water continues to come in through the broken window."

The C-130 pilot acknowledges the update and explains that this is the second C-130, and that they will drop a life raft and a pump.

The sailors move into the cockpit, awaiting the plane's approach. The C-130 roars low over the ocean, barely above the wave tops, and when it is over the *Almeisan* it is so close the trio can smell the plane's exhaust. A package is released from the plane with a long line attached to it. The line is meant to land on the sailboat, allowing the sailors to pull the package in. But, like the earlier air drops, the wind and seas are just too much; both package and line fall far wide of the boat and are engulfed by the seas.

A few minutes go by and the C-130 makes another low approach. This time the package does hit the boat, but then bounces off and is swept away before the crew can retrieve it.

The three sailors go below and gather by the radio. The C-130 pilot says that's enough of the gear dropping, the wind is just too strong. Then he says, "The motor vessel *Sakura Express,* a tanker, is coming to your aid. They are a few miles to your north. It will take them an hour to reach you in these seas. We have a helicopter refueling on board a Navy vessel, but it will be at least two hours before the helo can get to you. Do you want to try getting picked up by the tanker?"

It takes Ron, Kathy, and Chris only a minute to reach a unanimous decision to try for rescue with the tanker. The storm has not eased, and they all know what one big rogue wave will do to the *Almeisan.*

"Roger," says Ron. "We'll try for rescue with the tanker. When it arrives, I'll try to communicate directly with the captain."

Ron leaves the radio on, and a few minutes later the crew listens to the C-130 pilot talking to the tanker captain. And that's when they hear that the *Sakura Express* has already located the life raft but found it empty.

The three survivors share a glance. Kathy shakes her head slowly and looks down. No one says anything. They had all been hoping Loch and Tom were safe in the raft. Now they think their crewmates are surely dead: no one can survive in these savage seas for as long as they have been in the water—a full ten hours.

Besides determination, the only thing Loch and Tom have going for them is their ability to forestall hypothermia. Neither man feels particularly cold, but their muscles ache and burn because both are still kicking and paddling to hold position in the waves. Loch wonders how much more they can endure. He looks skyward and focuses on a single small patch of blue sky amidst the clouds and asks, *Will we ever be found?* He stares at the blue hole, fighting to keep his desperation from turning into capitulation. Then the clouds make a new shape within the blue sky area, and he swears it is speaking to him because the formation above looks exactly like the "OK" sign one makes with thumb and forefinger.

Buoyed by the message, he swims to Tom to share it, but sees that his friend is leaning over in the water toward his left side. Loch reaches out and lays a hand on Tom's shoulder, and Tom straightens as he reaches under his life vest and rubs his chest.

"Are you OK?" asks Loch.

Tom's face is haggard and ashen, making him look much older than his sixty-five years. Clearing his throat as best he can, he looks into Loch's eyes, saying, "It won't be long now, Yago."

In twenty years of friendship, Tom has never called Loch "Yago," and he wonders what it means. Loch is more concerned than ever.

Grabbing the collar of Tom's life vest, Loch tries to prop his friend up, shouting, "I'm here with you!"

Loch feels his hopes for rescue plummet, thinking, *We're just fooling ourselves about getting out of this.* He begins contemplating his own death and its effect on loved ones, especially his elderly mother. He pictures his wife, Sandy, driving to his mother's house on rural Rabbit Lane in Brookfield, Connecticut, and telling her of Loch's passing. It's almost more than he can bear. He stares at the clouds again, and this time he believes one of the clouds looks like the head of a rabbit sending him a message that his mom will be spared such news.

Loch wonders if the clouds are really sending him messages or if he's creating the images in his own mind, deciphering answers to keep himself going. Slowly an idea takes form. It doesn't matter if he's looking for meaning or answers from above, the clouds are providing him with positive feelings, and he instinctively knows that's the only way he will survive. He simply cannot let the negative thoughts take control, because he's felt their debilitating effects start to spread over him like a cancer. He vows then and there to use his thoughts to his advantage, and keep the image of eventual rescue first and foremost in his mind. As if to confirm his decision, he asks the sky how he will be rescued and as he looks upward he sees a cloud change shape and re-form into what looks like a helicopter. Loch smiles, knowing that whatever is happening above him or in his mind, it is helping him greatly.

A half hour passes with Loch doing his best to hold onto Tom's life vest collar. Every now and then he asks his friend how he's doing, and Tom gamely but weakly nods.

Tom's breathing is still labored and wheezing. Sometimes he gasps, struggling for air, and Loch holds tight to the collar, afraid Tom's head will simply drop face first into the sea. Loch suggests that he give Tom mouth-to-mouth resuscitation, but Tom shakes his head no.

Tom gathers a bit of strength and fumbles with the cord on his life vest. He doggedly works on the clamps, but finally stops, and instead motions for Loch to take his vest.

Loch cannot believe what Tom is doing. It's clear his friend thinks the end is near and he wants Loch to have the vest for extra buoyancy. Loch shakes his head. "No way. I need you with me. I promise I'll get you home."

Tom starts to smile but it turns into a violent convulsion, as he is unable to get air in his lungs.

Loch reacts in the only way he can, and tries giving Tom mouth-to-mouth. This seems to help, and Tom takes two shallow breaths. Then he stops breathing and his head drops. Again Loch blows air into his friend's lungs, silently thinking, *Come on, come on,* trying to will Tom to breathe by whatever means possible.

A minute goes by with Loch doing his best to breathe for Tom, but there is no response from his friend. *Don't die, don't die, you've come this far, just a little bit longer* . . . But Tom is gone, dead in Loch's arms.

CHAPTER NINETEEN

RUNNING OUT OF TIME

Around 3:30 p.m., Chris is in the cockpit and spots the *Sakura Express*. He shouts to Ron and Kathy, they join him topside, and all three watch the tanker lumber toward them through thirty- and forty-foot waves. The size of the tanker momentarily stuns the crew; at 590 feet in length it looks frighteningly huge, and the *Almeisan* feels smaller than ever as it pitches and plunges down from the foaming crests of waves smacking into the dark canyons below.

Chris, thinking the *Sakura Express* is Japanese rather than Panamanian, tries to break the tension. "Just think!" he shouts. "Once we're on board, we'll all be served sushi."

The comment gets a smile out of Ron and Kathy, but doesn't alleviate the concern about the tanker's size. It looks like a steel fortress bearing down on them.

The crew goes back below, and Ron makes radio contact with the *Sakura Express* captain, Srdan Tolja. The captain explains that they will fire a heaving line to the *Almeisan* and the survivors should tie it fast to the boat. The tanker will then pull alongside the sailboat and lower a basket to the deck, and the survivors should all get into the basket. If all goes well they will be immediately hoisted up to the tanker deck.

Chris and Kathy go up into the cockpit and watch the tanker pull within a hundred feet, towering above them. The rain is coming down harder than before, stinging their exposed faces as if they have been hit by a fistful of gravel. Chris clips his safety harness to the jackline on the port-side deck and looks up at the tanker's deck, where a crewmember is aiming the throw gun down at the sailboat. The deckhand fires the gun, but the wind blows the line wide of the *Almeisan's* stern. The tanker pulls closer, about fifty feet away. This time the deckhand uses his arm to throw the line and it sails directly over the sailboat, landing across its deck. Chris pulls it forward and ties it to the anchor windlass. Crewmembers on the *Sakura Express* are yelling and motioning wildly with their arms, but Chris doesn't understand what they want him to do. The tanker is now just twenty-five feet away.

The *Almeisan* is perpendicular to the starboard side of the *Sakura Express,* and a wave sends the sailboat surging, bow first, at the tanker. A terrible crack rings out as the *Almeisan's* bowsprit—a piece of solid mahogany, two feet long and eight inches thick—snaps like a matchstick. The impact sends Chris sprawling onto the foredeck, while Kathy is thrown to the deck in the cockpit, and Ron, below on the radio, is flung against the bulkhead.

The next wave sends the *Almeisan* rocketing back into the tanker, and Chris watches in horror as a deck joint buckles and the mainmast sways way beyond its normal range, indicating that the entire mast is coming loose.

A couple of more hits like this and the boat is going down, so Chris throws off the line connecting the two vessels. When he staggers back to the cockpit, Ron explains that the *Sakura Express* captain wanted him to haul in on the heaving line because it was attached to a much heavier mooring line.

Chris and Kathy go back out on the port side deck, and this time the *Sakura Express* deckhand is able to throw the heaving line directly into Chris's hands. Chris hauls in the line until he retrieves the mooring line, which he attaches to the anchor windlass.

Kathy has a sinking feeling: the steel hull of the ship looks like a giant hammer poised above the *Almeisan,* ready to strike.

The heavier mooring line makes little difference in the motion of the *Almeisan,* which crashes against the larger vessel, spiking up and down with the waves. Kathy and Chris step away from the port side in terror as an especially large wave shoots the *Almeisan* up from the waterline of the *Sakura Express* all the way to within ten feet of her deck, where anxious crewmembers are shouting encouragement. For a brief moment the decks of the two vessels are so close, the crews on each can look right into one another's eyes. Then the *Almeisan* plunges, scraping and banging against the hull of the tanker.

The deckhands aboard the *Sakura Express* start pulling on the heaving line, and the *Almeisan* moves forward along the tanker's hull, slamming into it each time a wave hits. Chris sees that the tanker crew has lowered a rope ladder, and they are pulling the sailboat to it. In a few seconds the sailboat is abreast of the ladder, and the ladder smacks the sailboat's deck when she rises on a wave. The ladder is now within Chris's reach, and he tenses his body, preparing to lunge for it.

Something holds him back, however. The two vessels are hammering into each other so hard he pictures his hands, gripping the ladder, being slammed against the tanker. If he loses his grip he will die, crushed between the two boats. But if he stays on the *Almeisan* he may meet the same fate. Then he thinks of Kathy and Ron, and abandons the thought of escaping the boat.

Again the tiny sailboat slams against the tanker and this time the port side spreader on the mizzenmast breaks free and crashes on the deck. Kathy's mind races: *This is crazy, we're going to be killed during a rescue attempt.*

The deckhands on the tanker have similar thoughts, and they release their end of the heaving line. The *Almeisan* careens free of the tanker's shadow.

Kathy and Chris unclip their tethers and decide the safest way to get from the forward deck back down into the cabin is to enter through the broken window. Once inside, they can't help but notice that there's more water in the vessel and bulkheads have shifted and broken.

Ron shouts from the radio, "What happened?"

Chris shouts back, "Tell the tanker to forget it, we're going to sink if we try that again!"

Ron radios the tanker captain: "We're getting beat up bad down here. There's no safe way to get off."

Captain Tolja responds, "I understand. We'll pull back and stand by. The U.S. Navy ship *Seay* is coming to your aid and there's a Coast Guard helicopter about to launch from the U.S. Navy ship *Trenton.*"

A few moments go by, and Chris climbs up the companionway and looks out the cockpit at the angry gray seas. It's raining so hard he can't even see the *Sakura Express,* though it is less than a half mile away. He looks at his watch. It's 4:30 p.m. *We're running out of time. If we don't get off this boat before dark, we're probably not going to make it.*

CHAPTER TWENTY

"I'VE GOT TO BRING HIM HOME"

After Tom breathed his last breath at 11 a.m., Loch just held his friend tight. He wasn't sure what to do, but decided to try and give Tom his last rites. He said a few words, prayed to God to take Tom's gentle spirit, and kissed him softly on the forehead. Then Loch cried.

Once he started he could not stop. Waves of grief swept over Loch, an aching pain much worse than any wave could throw at him. He wept uncontrollably, still clutching his friend, but utterly alone. His sobs were swept up by the wind and hurled into the void.

Now, in the afternoon, still tethered to Tom's lifeless body, still battered by the waves, Loch has time to think about the way his friend finally succumbed. It was as if Tom had decided that he was going to die with dignity, no matter what. Tom must have known that when the C-130 flew away the second time without seeing them, there would be no rescue anytime soon. He had done his best to fight the seas, but when he knew his time was near he tried to give Loch his life jacket.

Tom passed away with grace, thinks Loch. *He showed me how a brave man dies—stoic and uncomplaining. And now I've got to find a way to bring him home. I promised.*

Loch's fifty-eight-year-old body hurts all over. In the first couple of hours of the ordeal he would tense before each wave hit, and then when the wave drove him under, frantically fight his way back up to the surface. Now he realizes that approach is just wasting precious energy. He lets each wave crash upon him and relies on his life jacket to bring him to the surface, where he quickly orients himself so that his face is turned from the next oncoming seas. Mechanically, he sucks in two or three gulps of air, surveys the bleak surroundings for sign of a ship, and then is buried once more.

He looks like he's been mugged and left to suffer alone. Loch's neck and cheek have been rubbed raw by the life vest, and the chafing causes a trickle of blood to flow down through a growth of gray stubble on his skin. His face is drawn and haggard, his mouth dry and a bit swollen, and most painful of all are his bloodshot and salt-sore eyes. Whenever the sun breaks through the cloud cover, the stinging in his eyes is so severe he has to cover them with his arms, but he's afraid to close his eyes completely, worried he won't be able to get them back open, that they will simply be sealed shut.

What I would give for a pair of my daughter's swim goggles, Loch thinks. And he decides right then and there that on his next trip out on the ocean, his ditch bag will contain goggles.

On the surface, the thought seems absurd; he's already planning for his next trip! But he's tapping into his inner reserves, and convincing himself that despite the long odds, he will be rescued. He knows he's just a speck in the sea, but he's confident that the Coast Guard is implementing their rescue plan and giving it their all. *The only thing I can do is just hang on, and be ready when the Coast Guard comes. And they will come.*

This soft-spoken and unassuming man has a quiet yet steely determination, which few people would intuit upon meeting him. Certainly Loch's days in the military, albeit long ago, have helped forge his willpower and resolve, but even earlier than that he showed signs of being an independent and purposeful thinker with plenty of grit. When he was just fifteen years old he went to a summer camp in Ontario where his group made extended canoe trips on both rivers and lakes. The portages were the most grueling part of the journey. Several times he felt like giving up but realized that really wasn't an option because they were so far from civilization. From that canoe trip, Loch came to realize that he may not have been the fastest or strongest camper, but he had a stamina that surprised him. The trip gave him so much self-assurance that a year later, at age sixteen, he decided to simply hit the road with nothing more than a small backpack and head up into Canada alone. He began his odyssey by hitchhiking from Queens,

New York, to Buffalo, then on to Detroit. His backpack contained a change of clothes and a sleeping bag. Most nights he simply hiked into the woods off the highways, spread out his sleeping bag, and settled in for the night. He'd be up at dawn and be back on the road hitchhiking, eager to see what the new day would bring.

From Detroit he ventured north into the wilds of Michigan's Upper Peninsula, crossing into Canada at Sault Sainte Marie. The journey was totally unstructured and he loved every minute of it. Once in Canada, he had no specific destination, no timetable, and no one to meet. Usually he would simply pick a place on the map. *I think I'll go there.* Other times he'd get a ride, and the driver would ask, "Where are you headed?" Loch would answer with a question of his own: "Where are you going?" And when the driver responded, Loch would say, "I think I'll go there."

Loch wound up making a loop through a region of Ontario north of Lake Superior. First he traveled northeast to Timmons and then west through an isolated area of the province, before heading south to Thunder Bay, on the northwest shore of Lake Superior. The final leg of his journey found him hitching rides due east for several hundred miles, passing through North Bay and Kingston, Ontario, and ultimately returning to the States via upstate New York.

Besides feeling the thrill of seeing new places, meeting new people, and having a sense of total freedom, Loch also grew in confidence, knowing he could tackle just about any problem that life on the road could throw at him. And just as with his earlier canoe trip, he knew he had stamina to get through physically demanding situations. This staying power, as well as his newfound feeling of resourcefulness, were just two of the reasons he later gravitated to rigorous and demanding blue-water sailing.

And now, battered by the seas, minutes seeming like hours, Loch needs every bit of internal toughness he can muster. His mind drifts to places he really doesn't want it to go. He wonders if Kathy, Ron, and Chris are alive, thinking that if they have drowned and he lives, he must explain to their families what went wrong. This thought leads to the feeling that he let them down, particularly when he recalls how at the beginning of the storm he and Tom forgot to install the protective shutters called "dead lights" over the two large windows above the *Almeisan*'s settee. The storm shutters were on the boat, but in the confusion—coupled with his own seasickness—he simply overlooked that safety step.

Next he thinks of his family, wondering if he will ever again watch his thirteen-year-old daughter play softball. Then he catches himself. *Stop, don't even think that way. I am going to make it. My family is depending on me, and so is Tom's.* He looks over at Tom's lifeless body floating five feet away, and renews his vow to bring his friend home. That single thought gives him a focus to concentrate on the now and not on the past. And right now his eyes hurt so much he decides to do something unorthodox and risky: he lowers his head into the ocean and opens his eyes, rinsing them in the very water that has caused so much pain. Amazingly, it helps, perhaps because the water rinses away some of the built-up salt. As he's refocusing his vision, relieved to be able to see a bit more clearly, he turns to his left and suddenly stops, his mouth agape. For a brief second, while atop a wave, he sees what he thinks is the gray hull of a ship less than half a mile away. The next wave buries him and when he rises back up he squints into the distance, and this time there can be no mistake: it is a ship. Frantically Loch waves his yellow ditch bag for all he's worth.

After five exhausting minutes of signaling he drops his weary arm. The ship is moving, from left to right; no one on board spotted him.

It's a bitter sight to watch the vessel disappear into the gloom, and Loch wonders why he didn't notice the ship earlier. First he thinks it's because of his salt-strained eyes, but as he reconsiders the situation he realizes that he had conditioned himself to be looking forward, away from the towering waves, and this ship had come from behind. He curses himself, thinking that if he had spotted the ship earlier, he might have been able to swim in a line that would bring him closer to the approaching vessel, and maybe the crew would have seen him.

He doesn't dwell on the mistake for long, instead telling himself, *You've got to always be ready. Every time I'm at the top of a wave I've got to spin around and look in every direction.* Even more important, he gets back to talking to himself in a positive way. *I'm going to make it. That ship had to be looking for me. Don't give up. Tom died only a short while before that ship appeared. Help could come at any moment. Just fight a little longer.*

CHAPTER TWENTY-ONE

THE *SEAY*

Portsmouth Search and Rescue has learned the identity of the three people on board the *Almeisan,* and because two of them are from New England, the search coordinator contacts District 1 in Boston: "We need you to be up on the case details to field any calls from the families."

District 1 responds: "Roger. Also understand you may need us to do NOK [Next of Kin] since the people are from up in the New England area. But we will await tasking."

Portsmouth also now knows that the *Sakura Express* rescue attempt has been aborted and they are anxious for the *Trenton* to bring the helicopter close enough to the *Almeisan* so it can launch. Portsmouth is worried about running out of daylight, saying in one message that the *Almeisan*'s situation is "getting dicey."

Fortunately, a Navy transport ship, the *Seay,* is only three miles from the *Almeisan.* Because the ship has a crane and a rescue boat, Portsmouth thinks they will be more successful than the *Sakura Express* in a rescue attempt. The *Seay* is given the green light to try and save the sailboat crew.

On board the *Almeisan,* Chris, Ron, and Kathy are not sure what's going to happen next, but they are thankful they have radio communications with the C-130 above. For the first time since the knockdown they are worried their vessel could capsize even without being hit by a rogue wave. The battering during the *Sakura Express* rescue attempt has made the vessel more fragile than ever as it wallows in the heaving, wind-raked seas. They soon learn via the radio that the *Seay* will try a rescue, or at least create a lee sea by acting as a shield against oncoming waves. The three survivors, however, are on edge, thinking of their close call with the *Sakura Express*. Chris goes up into the cockpit to await the ship and notices that the howling wind is stronger than before. Visibility is down to a half mile. Rain continues to fall in torrents, blurring the distinction between water and sky.

Out of the gloom comes the *Seay*. It is even larger than the *Sakura Express*, almost double its size, at 950 feet in length. To Chris, the Navy ship looks like a colossal iceberg bearing down on them. Conversely, the *Almeisan* looks like a child's toy to the *Seay* crewmembers looking down.

Slowly the *Seay* approaches the *Almeisan's* stern, but despite its careful advance the massive ship sends out a bow wave that crests and breaks over the *Almeisan,* causing Chris to duck in the cockpit. Within seconds, however, the ship is alongside the *Almeisan's* port side, and the *Seay's* captain, Thomas Madden, does an amazing job matching his speed to the drifting sailboat. Now the *Almeisan* is in the lee of the ship and for the first time in over twenty-four hours the seas become manageable ten-foot swells. Chris relaxes with relief.

Ron has established radio contact with *Seay's* radio operator and is told that a line will be tossed down from the ship. The idea is for the line to be secured to the *Almeisan,* which will hold them to the side of the *Seay* until the Coast Guard helicopter arrives for the rescue. The seas are simply too rough to risk using the *Seay's* crane to pluck out the survivors or using the ship's small launch. Ron passes the information on to Kathy, who in turn climbs up the companionway and tells Chris.

The *Seay* crew doesn't have to throw the line because the *Almeisan* is directly below them. They simply lower a heaving line that Chris fastens to the port side midship cleat, just outside the cockpit. The *Almeisan* collides with the *Seay,* but not as violently as with the *Sakura Express.* As the sailboat drifts aft of the ship, it appears the plan is a good one—until the *Almeisan* hits a torrent of water being discharged from the side of the ship. The stream of water floods the cockpit, knocking Chris off his feet, then gushes belowdecks through the blown window. Chris, shocked but still functioning, scrambles to his feet and unties the heaving line before the *Almeisan* sinks.

The two vessels are so close to one another that the *Almeisan* slides along the *Seay*'s hull until it reaches the stern, where it is sucked in tight, directly under the enormous ship's curved stern. Chris is absolutely terrified as a wall of gray metal plunges down toward the cockpit. He dives for cover in the deck of the cockpit, hears the metal columns holding up the hardtop above him start to crack, and fears he's going to be crushed to death. A sharp crash fills the air, and the mizzenmast, aft of the mainmast, splinters at its base and slams onto the deck.

Below, Ron and Kathy stagger as the *Almeisan* makes a sudden lurch downward, the impact so severe that cabinets topple from their mountings. More water floods the boat and for the first time in the entire storm, Ron thinks this might be it.

Suddenly, the *Seay*'s hull gives the *Almeisan* a bit of breathing room. Chris sneaks a peak out the cockpit but all he can see is foaming water and the gray hull of the ship. Just a few feet below and forward spin the giant twin propellers of the *Seay*.

The hull of the ship once again looks like it's going to squash the boat and Chris screams to Kathy and Ron, "We're going to get hit again! Get ready to abandon ship!"

Then the *Almeisan* shoots backward and they are free of the *Seay*'s hull. The *Seay* eases off and tries to create the lee sea from a safer distance.

Chris climbs below and the three shaken survivors crowd around the radio.

"I thought we were going down," says Kathy. "I was sure we would all be crushed."

"We were being crushed!" shouts Chris. "It's an absolute mess topside. Even the hardtop is shattered."

"And I think our hull is cracked," says Ron. He pauses, first rubbing his hand over the egg-size contusion on his forehead, and then strokes his short gray beard. "We've just got to hang in there until the helicopter arrives. I guess the sea doesn't give things up easily."

Chris thinks about this last comment and asks himself, *Does someone not want us to get out of here?*

About the same time Chris is wondering if they will be saved before the boat sinks, Lieutenant Commander Bader, on board the *Trenton*, receives clearance that he and his crew can launch their helicopter. He quickly locates his copilot, Audie Andry, who is on the deck, hugging the rail, looking off toward the gray horizon. Noting that Andry looks almost as green as the sea, Bader says, "Are you sure you can do this?"

"Once we get airborne I'll be fine," croaks Andry. "I can't wait to get off this ship."

Bader pauses, thinking the situation over, then slaps Andry on the back, saying, "Good, because we just got clearance to launch."

The plan calls for Bader and crew to take off immediately, because pitch and roll limits are borderline, and the seas are increasing. Once at the emergency scene they will airlift the survivors off the *Almeisan* and then fly to Nantucket, the nearest land-based airport. Returning to the ship is not a viable option because of nightfall and the worsening conditions.

The helicopter crew, consisting of Lieutenant Commander Eric Bader, copilot Audie Andry, rescue swimmer A. J. Thompson, and flight mechanic James Geramita, goes through a final briefing then boards the aircraft. They power up the rotors and take off into the wind, expecting to reach the *Almeisan* in just over thirty minutes. As he predicted, Andry feels his nausea disappear immediately, and he gives a thumbs-up sign to Bader, confident that they can pull this rescue off.

His sense of well-being doesn't last long. Checking the helicopter's electronic navigation system against the magnetic compass, Andry realizes they are forty-five degrees off course. He tries adjusting various controls with no luck and explains the situation to the flight commander.

When Bader hears the news he thinks, *Let's see, we're more than two hundred miles offshore, heading into bad weather, and our navigation system is messed up. Not a good start.*

While Andry continues troubleshooting, Bader contacts the C-130 circling the *Almeisan,* explaining that it might be necessary for the plane to fly to the helicopter and lead them to the sailboat. He says for now he and his crew will try to reach the emergency scene using the magnetic compass. Bader figures that he'll reach the *Almeisan* one way or another, but his real concern is getting to Nantucket after the

115

rescue. It will be dark and he must keep the helicopter's altitude low to conserve fuel, while the C-130, which will escort them, will be flying significantly higher to give them more breathing room from the water. (The wingspan on a C-130 is close to a hundred feet, and the pilots want to allow plenty of space for banking without worrying about hitting the crest of the waves.)

Several minutes go by—minutes that really can't be spared, with night coming on—and still the navigation system does not work. Precious gallons of fuel are being wasted as they drone off course. Bader decides to ask the C-130 to come to his position.

Neither Bader nor Andry understands why the navigation system is malfunctioning, but Andry decides to handle it the same way many of us deal with personal computer problems; shut it down and then restart. When the system powers back up, however, it is still giving incorrect data, and Andry—who almost never curses—swears loudly at the glowing navigation screen. He tries a couple of more corrective actions, but the system doesn't respond, and partly out of frustration he again turns the system off. A couple of minutes later he restarts it and this time it's functioning fine.

Ironically, the C-130 arrives shortly after the navigation system begins to work. Although the plane is no longer needed to guide them, Bader turns the situation to his advantage after learning that the two men piloting the plane are former helicopter pilots who understand exactly what he's up against. Bader asks for and gets a detailed review of the on-scene conditions, status of the persons on board the sinking boat, and a summary of the rescue attempts by the *Sakura Express* and the *Seay*. They discuss the role and proximity of the *Seay* to the sailboat, and all the pilots conclude that it's best to have the Navy ship back off a bit farther from the *Almeisan,* so that the helicopter pilot will have unimpeded room for the rescue. With thirty- and forty-foot seas, blasting wind, and poor visibility, the last thing a helicopter pilot needs to worry about is being blown into a huge ship whose superstructure will be higher than the height of the helicopter.

As the helicopter heads farther into the storm, wind gusts exceed fifty knots, putting further strain on their fuel supply. The rain picks up, pelting the aircraft, as if warning the crew that they're entering a place where nature, not mechanics, rules. Bader and Andry recalculate their fuel situation and set their "bingo time"—the last exact moment at which they absolutely must leave the rescue scene and head back to Nantucket. They estimate that once they arrive at the *Almeisan* they will have only twenty-five minutes to complete the evacuation of the three stranded sailors. When those twenty-five minutes are up, they leave, no matter what, even if they have not rescued all the sailors, and even if their rescue swimmer is still in the water. If they push the bingo time up, the helicopter will likely not make it to Nantucket, and they will all end up in the water, dead.

In the cabin of the aircraft, rescue swimmer A. J. Thompson notices that with each passing mile, visibility is decreasing due to cloud cover and the approach of evening. The helicopter is now experiencing some turbulence, and he and flight mechanic Geramita exchange glances as the aircraft takes some punches. A.J. looks at the sea spray below, where the wind is shearing the tops off enormous waves. His adrenaline is already pumping as he prepares himself for what's to come. He's thinking of different scenarios he might encounter, and running through his responses to the challenges. The one scenario he does not dwell on is being left alone in the ocean, but it is a risk that rescue swimmers face. Once a rescue swimmer detaches from the cable in the water, there's no guarantee he is going to get back to land.

CHAPTER TWENTY-TWO

MAKE SOME LUCK

Islands of foam hurl through the air as the sea and the wind do battle. Alone, caught in the middle of the chaos, Loch wonders how much more he can take. It's late afternoon and the weather has turned fouler, the ocean grayer, and the rain more steady. It appears the storm is intensifying rather than weakening.

It seems that every bit of bad luck possible—both prior to being swept overboard and after—has befallen the besieged sailor. Still, his predicament could be far worse if he were floating on the northwest side of the Gulf Stream, where water temperatures are in the upper 50s and low 60s rather than his current position at the Gulf Stream's eastern edge, with temperatures in the lower 70s. These warmer waters can still be lethal, but it may take a whole day rather than hours for a person to expire.

So far, Loch is fending off hypothermia better than most people could, defying odds predicting that at this stage of his fight—thirteen hours in the water—he should be unconscious or unable to function in any meaningful way. His only symptoms are stiff muscles. He doesn't yet feel particularly cold. A bigger anguish is dehydration, which is adding to his crushing fatigue.

Every time Loch rides high on a wave, he continues to look in all directions, determined not to miss spotting a ship. Now, however, his gaze also scans the nearby waters. For the first time during his ordeal he's thinking about sharks, and he instinctively tries to be as still as possible. He knows that his yellow foul-weather suit is the type of color that might attract a shark, but it's also the bright color that a searcher in a plane just might distinguish from the white and gray waves.

The Hardin forty-five-foot-long *Almeisan* had two masts; the forward mast was the taller of the two.

A bird's-eye view of the *Almeisan* during calm seas.

Captain Tom Tighe, age sixty-five, had
made forty-eight crossings between
Connecticut and Bermuda.

First mate Lochlin Reidy, fifty-eight years old, had made
several blue-water voyages with Tom Tighe.

Ron Burd, age seventy, was a retired engineer who owned his own sailboat.

Kathy Gilchrist, age forty-six, loved sailing and had spent many hours at sea.

Crewmember Chris Ferrer was a thirty-four-year-old molecular biologist and information technology administrator. He owned his own sailboat and wanted to learn more about offshore sailing.

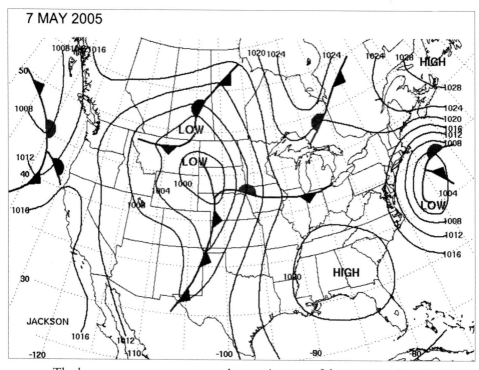

The low-pressure system covered a massive area of the ocean on May 7.

The Coast Guard helicopter flight crew. *From left to right:* A. J. Thompson, Donald Eric Bader, Audie Andry, James Geramita.

Pilot Audie Andry by the helicopter's cabin door.

Tom Tighe is shown in foul-weather gear during heavy weather several years before the accident. He is carefully making his way from the bow aft to the cockpit.

The salon area, with its bench and table, was directly below a large window.

The orange-hulled *Sakura Express* was
a 590-foot-long oil tanker.

A view of the Almeisan from the Navy ship *Seay*.
Note the missing window on the sailboat.

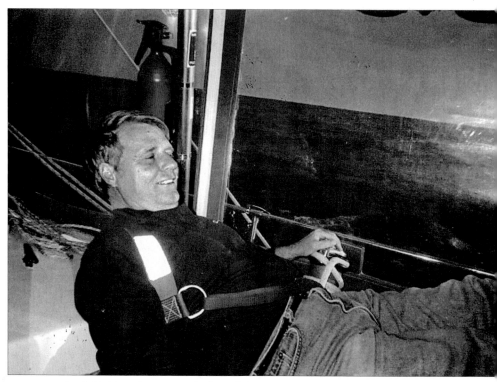
Loch Reidy relaxing on deck. Safety harnesses were always worn when on deck in heavy weather and at night.

The Gulf Stream's warm temperatures certainly allow for more species of sharks to be patrolling its waters, but the kind Loch is most worried about is the mako, both the short-fin and long-fin mako; the latter can grow to thirteen feet in length and weigh 1,400 pounds. Both makos are fast, and the short-fin is said to be able to reach bursts of speed topping thirty-five miles per hour and jump close to twenty feet out of the water. Neither is the shy, retiring type, and more than one mako, having been hooked by an angler, has jumped out of the water and into the boat, fighting its tormenters in the cockpit. And in rare instances, a mako has freed itself from the hook, only to come back and ram the boat. The International Game Fish Association says the short-fin mako is "the undisputed leader in attacks on boats."

But as he looks around at the churning seas, he thinks, *No shark in its right mind would be swimming near the surface in these conditions.* This thought is not just wishful thinking; it's likely that the turbulent water would make it difficult for a shark to detect Loch's movements. Sharks can sense vibrations in the water from long distances, but in a storm like this the whole surface of the ocean is one big boiling mass of motion, and sharks probably avoid it.

Loch's attention turns from scanning the water for fins to listening to a strange hissing sound. He looks around for the source of the noise that sounds a bit like steam escaping, and seeing nothing, his mind races. *Could it be a fish? A shark? Could it be the wind?* A minute or two goes by and Loch begins to wonder if he's imagining the noise, and if so whether it means he's losing his grip on reality. But the hissing sound is real, and Loch smiles when he discovers the seemingly benign source. When the waves break on him all matter of foam surrounds him, and within this foam are millions of tiny bubbles, bursting around his head. He questions why he is just noticing the sound now, but has no answer.

Taking his mind off sharks and foam, Loch decides to do an inventory of his ditch bag. His shoulders slump as he realizes his bag has somehow opened; gone are his wallet, passport, money, and GMT Rolex. The loss of his watch especially upsets him because it makes him think of his family. The day that he purchased his watch, he also purchased one for his wife, Sandy, and his older daughter,

Denise. He pictures his watch plummeting to the bottom of the ocean, thousands of fathoms below him. If he doesn't try to make some luck of his own, he will be in the same place, never to see his family again.

With that thought he starts to go through Tom's bug-out bag, where he finds a metal reflecting mirror and two glow sticks. Loch puts them in the pocket of his jacket, so he can get at the items quickly should a plane or ship appear. Next he searches Tom's jacket and finds a handheld six-inch radio transmitter. For a second his spirits soar, but then realizes the receiver is full of water and useless. Tom must have stuffed it in his pocket as he was preparing to abandon ship, hoping that it might transmit a short distance from inside the raft.

A wave washes over Loch, and when he comes to the surface he decides that with nightfall approaching it's time to test the combination flashlight and strobe light attached to each man's safety harness. Each harness also has a knife, and Loch uses his own knife to cut the lights off. First he severs his light so that he can hold it, and turns the switch on. Nothing happens. Then he cuts Tom's light free, and it too does not work. *How many more setbacks can I take?*

He's got to fight down the rising frustration and alarm, but a sense of terrible dread envelops him as he thinks about being alone in the water in the dark. *Calm down, just keep doing your best.*

After the next wave cascades over Loch, he decides to use the relative stillness on the back side of the wave to examine one of the lights more closely. There's a flashlight on one end and a strobe on the other, with batteries in between. He carefully unscrews the cylinder and removes the batteries, clutching them tightly. Another wave pounds him, but he holds onto both the light and the batteries. He quickly pours the water out of the light, shaking it hard, hoping to move the contact points. Then he inserts the batteries and screws the cylinder as tight as possible. Another wave smacks him on the back of the head, dunking him. When he surfaces he turns the switch on. Both the flashlight and the strobe work. Loch almost cries in relief. *OK, that's your first big break. Now fix the other one.* And so he does. Both lights go into the pocket of his foul-weather gear and he seals it shut with a Velcro strip.

As he removes his hand from his pocket a yellow one-inch object floats free from his sleeve. He recoils from it, thinking it's some kind of leech. A wave lands on Loch, and when he surfaces the leech is gone. He scans the water around him looking for more but doesn't see any. After convincing himself that this is a onetime occurrence, Loch relaxes a bit. A couple of minutes go by. Then out from under his rain gear cuff comes another yellow leech, which Loch quickly grabs and flips away. He's appalled that more of the strange creatures have gotten inside his clothes, and thinks, *Here I am in the middle of the ocean in a killer storm and I've got to worry about leeches crawling on my body.* He recalls how when he was a boy, swimming in a pond, two leeches attached themselves to his skin, and how disgusted he was by the sensation and sight. He's got that same feeling now.

More time goes by and yet another leech floats up from his jacket. This time he snatches it firmly and brings it close to his eyes. Loch shakes his head. It's not a leech at all but a piece of lining from the inside of his foul-weather jacket that was shredded by the waves and came free. He manages a grim smile. *Another mystery solved. At least it took my mind off the fix I'm in.*

Loch is now practicing a breathing routine where he takes short little breaths in wave troughs and large gulps of air at the top. Every fiber in his body cries out with exhaustion, and his weary mind feels sluggish from sleep deprivation. *No wonder I thought pieces of my coat were leeches. I've just got to take things slow.* To conserve energy he does not try to spin around at the top of each wave to look for ships but instead limits that effort to every third wave. He's also staying close to Tom's body, often leaning on it for support.

How am I going to make it through another twelve hours in the dark? He answers his own question: *You've just got to do it. They're never going to find you at night. Rescue will come in the daylight, so just get through these next twelve hours.*

Worried about his ebbing strength, Loch removes some of the seaweed he had earlier stuffed in his pocket. He remembers how Tom shook his head and smiled when Loch was gathering it. *Well, Tom, you'd really laugh now, because I'm going to eat it.*

He shoves a piece of seaweed into his mouth. The taste is absolutely awful; oily, coarse, and salty. Loch gags, trying to chew. He can't bring himself to swallow it and spits it out.

As the minutes go by and the waves keep coming an idea comes to Loch. He inflates the two ditch bags, and using the rope loops attached to them, he ties one to each of Tom's ankles. This will raise more of Tom's body to the surface, making a bigger target for rescuers to see. He recalls Tom making it clear that passengers on the *Almeisan* must have yellow or orange foul-weather gear, no trendy white, blue, or green. Tom knew that if anyone went overboard, yellow and orange were the best colors to stand out.

Loch puts both his arms up on Tom's torso, using Tom as a float. He has the fleeting feeling that Tom's spirit is helping him. But as afternoon gives way to evening, the sense of loneliness is all but overwhelming.

CHAPTER TWENTY-THREE

THE FAMILIES

When the *Almeisan*'s EPIRB went off and the Coast Guard called Tom's logistician, Donna Christman, it was 3:50 a.m. Sunday morning, Mother's Day. Donna was already awake, pacing the floors, unable to sleep, knowing from her last conversation with Tom that the sailboat was in the grip of rough weather. She also knew, just from the tone of Tom's voice during the call, that the weather had already taken a toll on him, and perhaps had damaged the boat. He had given her his longitude and latitude, but told her he was too busy to go into details about the storm; he would get back to her later.

The Coast Guard informed her about the activation of the EPIRB, and asked if Tom could have been testing it. "No way," Donna almost shouted, "I am telling you they must be in deep trouble. They were in a storm when I spoke to him last, around eight p.m."

After updating the Coast Guard with all the information she had, Donna made a call to Anne Tighe, Tom's wife. The number Donna called was Anne's cell phone, and she left her a message to call her right away because the Coast Guard had received a signal from the *Almeisan*'s EPIRB.

It wasn't until midmorning that Anne turned her cell phone on and realized there was a voice message. As she listened to the message, Anne's heart skipped a beat. She immediately called Donna back, but Donna didn't have any additional news. Anne called the Coast Guard. A spokesperson said that a Coast Guard plane was already at the *Almeisan*'s location, and that initial reports indicated the captain and first mate were in a life raft and the other three people were still on board the sailboat. Upon hearing that, Anne said, "That can't be right. Tom and Loch would never just leave the others."

The next few hours were a roller coaster of emotion, with Anne clinging to the hope that whatever had happened, maybe Tom and Loch were indeed safe in the life raft. Then she got the phone call that sent her spirits plunging. She was informed that a vessel named the *Sakura Express* had located the life raft but it was empty. Now she knew the two men were in the ocean, and that the C-130s had so far been unable to find them.

As evening approached, Anne felt her despair increasing with each hour, knowing what the waves and hypothermia can do to someone adrift in a storm.

Sue Burd, Ron's wife, had been tracking the low-pressure system online since Friday, and had an uneasy feeling because the storm was so enormous. She was in contact with Donna on Saturday, and Donna reported that although they were making slow progress in rough weather, everything was OK. On Sunday Sue had to fly to a business conference in Atlanta, and Donna tried to reach her while she was in the air. Sue didn't turn on her cell phone until she had boarded a cab outside the Atlanta airport—that's when she listened to the voice message from Donna that said, "There's been an accident. The EPIRB went off on the *Almeisan*. The Coast Guard says there are two people in a life raft, and three souls on the boat. Call me when you get this message."

Sue sat in the cab, stunned, thinking, *This can't be real.* She immediately called Donna, who said the Coast Guard thought that the captain and first mate were the ones in the life raft. But both Sue and Donna thought the information must be wrong, that the crew would never split up like that.

When Sue arrived at the hotel she called family members, and they in turn tried to learn all they could by going online. They found an earlier press release from the Coast Guard that said the captain and first mate had "abandoned" the boat and were in a life raft while the other three crewmembers were on the boat. Again Sue thought that couldn't be correct. But one part of her wanted to believe it, because she knew that Ron would be one of the people on the boat. The couple had sailed together for years, talked about what to do in emergencies, and Ron was firm in his conviction that you never leave the boat until you are positive it's going down.

Later that afternoon Sue's daughter called her and said that the press release had been modified. She explained the word *abandoned* had been removed from the announcement. Sue's daughter then asked, "What if they changed the press release because they don't really know who is on the boat and who is in the water?" Now Sue was really rattled, but she told her daughter, "Ron would never leave the boat. He's got to be one of the people on it." But deep inside Sue wasn't so sure. She finally got through to the Coast Guard, and they explained they could not yet confirm who was in the boat. Then they broke the news that the life raft had been found, empty. It was then that Sue gripped the cell phone so hard she broke it.

The stakes were higher than ever now. There could be loss of life. Being hundreds of miles away from her family made the situation more stressful. Sue wasn't sure whether or not to fly home or stay put, and so she waited in her room, sitting by the hotel phone, wondering if Ron was still alive.

Laura Ferrer, Chris's wife, was also caught away from home and on the road when she first learned of the accident. Five months pregnant, Laura had driven earlier from Massachusetts to Pennsylvania to attend a baby shower hosted by her mother and friends. She was driving back home Sunday afternoon when her cell phone rang. Looking down at the caller ID display, she knew it was Donna calling. Laura had a bad feeling and was reluctant to talk to Donna. She waited a minute, then played the voice message back. "This is Donna Christman calling. I heard from the Coast Guard this morning. The boat is in some trouble and the EPIRB has gone off. I'll call again when I receive more news."

Laura almost wrecked the car. She was expecting information about the voyage being delayed due to weather, but certainly not this. Pulling the car over to the shoulder of the highway, she called Donna back, hoping for more specific details. Donna explained that she didn't have much information, only that the Coast Guard was on the way to the boat's location.

Laura was about an hour away from a close friend's house, and she called that friend, telling her what she had just learned. Her friend, a spiritual person, told Laura to drive straight to her house, while she got busy calling a network of friends and family members, asking them to pray.

When Laura arrived at her friend's home, she called Chris's parents and broke the news. Chris's mom had urged Chris not to go on the voyage because she had recently read about the cruise ship the *Norwegian Dawn* being struck by a rogue wave while in the Gulf Stream. Now her fears had come true, and both women broke down sobbing.

Sandy Reidy, Loch's wife, was one of the last family members to learn about the accident. That Sunday, being Mother's Day, she and her youngest daughter, Ashley, had been away all day visiting her daughter Denise in New Jersey. She and Ashley did not return home until 10 p.m. Upon entering her house, she noticed the light on her phone's answering machine blinking. There were two messages. The first one she listened to was short and cryptic: "This is WTNH-TV calling, please return our call as soon as possible."

What in the world, Sandy wondered, *is that all about?* Then she listened to the other message and knew the answer. The second message was equally short, saying that Mrs. Reidy should immediately call the U.S. Coast Guard in Boston.

Sandy felt the blood drain from her face as she dialed the number given to her. The Coast Guard spokesperson broke the news that her husband, Loch, and captain Tom Tighe were missing at sea. Because it was 10 p.m., and the rescue had been under way for some time, the Coast Guard was able to give her a detailed summary of the rescue efforts, while also informing her that the two men had likely been in the water for eighteen hours.

Sandy thanked the Coast Guardsman, collapsed on the sofa, and just stared outside her windows into the black night, thinking of Loch adrift in the ocean.

Not a sailor herself, Sandy was never entirely comfortable with Loch's making his yearly voyage, but this year, both before and after her husband left, she felt particularly anxious. Now she was stunned, struggling with the unreal feeling that in the last five minutes her world had been turned upside down. She then called her daughter Denise.

Denise had made two Bermuda voyages on the *Almeisan* with Loch and Tom, so of all the family members, she was the most familiar with the challenges of this blue-water trip. She alone also knew how much Loch enjoyed sailing, how he was thrilled and energized by the experience, and how he seemed more at home on the sea than he did on land. Denise was aware of the dangers, the perils, and the discomforts of such a lengthy voyage. She was not, however, prepared for her mother's call.

Denise listened as Sandy reiterated what the Coast Guard said, explaining that Loch and Tom were in the ocean, and that the three other crewmembers were still on the *Almeisan*.

"Something is not right with this story," said Denise to her mother, recovering from the initial shock of the news. "There is no way that Loch and Tom would ever leave that boat without the others. Those two would be the last ones off, not the first."

Denise then told Sandy that she and her husband would drive from their New Jersey home to Connecticut to be with her. As soon as she hung up the phone, however, Denise called the Coast Guard. The Coast Guard confirmed that Loch and Tom were indeed overboard, but they did not know how it happened. Denise asked for a summary of what was going to happen next, along with the prognosis for a successful search. She needed to hear the details herself from the Coast Guard, before she saw her mother.

There was silence for a moment on the other end of the line before she got her answer. "Here's the scenario," said the Coast Guard representative. "Imagine taking two coconuts out on a plane and dropping them in the middle of the ocean. Then fly back to land. Wait twenty-four hours. Then fly back out to sea and try to find them in the middle of a storm."

Denise now had the confirmation she needed to understand what they were up against.

PART III

CHAPTER TWENTY-FOUR

THE CABLE

Ron, Kathy, and Chris are gathered by the radio, still shaken from their encounter with the fantail of the *Seay*. It is 5:45 p.m. and the boat is in complete shambles. Topside, rigging hangs from the deck next to the crushed hardtop, while below, cupboards, debris, floorboards, and all manner of gear slosh about in the seawater inside the vessel. Kathy had felt the *Almeisan* could survive the beating of enormous waves, but no longer. The battered boat is listing and sluggish. She fears all it will take is one good-size wave to lay the vessel flat and it simply won't come back up.

Suddenly the radio crackles to life. Lieutenant Commander Bader, piloting the helicopter, is calling for the *Almeisan,* and Ron answers. Bader says, "We are approximately ten minutes away from you. We are going to go over the evacuation procedures now, because we are low on fuel and we've got to do the rescue fast."

Bader explains that they will be lowering their rescue swimmer, and the swimmer will then give them instructions on when to jump from the *Almeisan* and into the sea, where he will assist them in getting into the rescue basket. Bader tells Ron that they need to decide the order in which each survivor will be taken off.

Ron immediately answers back, "Kathy will go first, Chris second, and me last."

Kathy objects, saying it would be better to simply draw straws and that Ron shouldn't have to be last.

"Sorry," says Ron with a smile, "I've got seniority on this one."

During the ten-minute wait for the helicopter, the survivors double-check the snugness of their PFDs and make sure they have their ditch bags with their passports and wallets. Kathy grabs the boat's logbook and stuffs it into her bug-out bag. They are so anxious to get off the *Almeisan* that the thought of jumping into thirty-foot seas causes only minor concern. All three crewmembers feel that if they don't board the helicopter before dark they probably won't live through the night. They resolve that when the rescue swimmer says to jump, they will do so without a moment's hesitation.

"Listen," says Ron, holding a hand up. First faint, then louder, and finally earsplitting is the *whop, whop, whop, whop* of the helicopter's rotor blades drowning out the background sound of crashing waves.

Flight mechanic and hoist operator James Geramita is looking down on the *Almeisan* as the helicopter descends from 300 feet to just 100 feet above the enraged ocean. He is in awe of the seas. Never has he seen waves this large. With the *Almeisan* providing contrast, his depth perception has improved from when he gazed at the seas during the flight, and the waves appear bigger than the earlier reports of twenty- to thirty-footers. And they are. The altimeter at the bottom of the aircraft frequently goes from 100 feet to 60 feet as a wave top comes up toward the helicopter, indicating that there are some 40-foot waves below. He can't imagine what the people in the sailboat are going through, but he's certain they are bruised—no one would be able to keep their footing in such instability. Geramita's heart is pounding, knowing that the lives of the survivors, as well as that of rescue swimmer A. J. Thompson, will be in his hands in the coming minutes.

Geramita also knows that direct deployment of A.J. onto the sailboat would be suicidal. The violent motion of the sailboat, with its two masts and rigging shooting upward near the top of each wave, then pitching over to a forty-five-degree angle when the wave breaks on the boat, creates a deadly hazard. Instead he's got to get the swimmer safely in the water, and he begins visualizing how he's going to do that without having a wave bury A.J. before he even has a chance to unhook.

A.J. is suited up in dry suit, gloves, harness, and fins. Before he takes his helmet off, with its built-in radio, he and Geramita review the plan one last time. "Get me as close as possible to the sailboat, or I'll never reach it!" says A.J. Both men know that the sailboat, with its large surface area, will be pushed by the wind much faster than the rescue swimmer will drift. A.J. will have to use a short burst of swimming speed to catch the fast-moving sailboat.

The two men discuss how A.J. will be lowered on the cable to a spot just aft of the boat's stern, then swim to the boat. If he can climb aboard he will do so; if not, he'll motion for the first survivor to jump into the water.

A.J. removes his helmet, puts his hood on, adjusts his mask and snorkel, then nods to Geramita that he's ready to go. The twenty-six-year-old hoist operator tells the pilots he's deploying the swimmer. He will tell the pilots exactly what he's doing each moment, acting as the pilots' eyes and ears with regard to both the swimmer and the survivors.

A.J. attaches the hook at the end of the cable to his harness and leans out of the open doorway until he is in the air.

Geramita slowly lowers him, pausing when A.J. is near the sea, waiting to place him on the back side of a wave so the swimmer will have time to unhook in the trough before the next comber rolls over him.

As soon as A.J. hits the water he unhooks and swims toward the sailboat with every ounce of strength. A minute goes by and A.J. realizes he's not gaining on the boat at all. He swims with renewed effort, but after another thirty seconds it's clear he's losing this race. As feared, the sailboat is being pushed by the wind faster than A.J. can swim.

A.J. stops, looks up at the Jayhawk, and gives the thumbs-up sign, which indicates to Geramita that he needs to be picked up. He is sucking in both air and foam, and inside his dry suit, sweat is dripping from his pores like rain. A wet suit might have been a better choice for a quick rescue in the Gulf Stream, but if for some reason A.J. gets stranded in the water, the dry suit might just save his life. Then too, no one knew if the sailboat would still be drifting along the eastern edge of the Gulf Stream or in the colder waters to the west by the time the helicopter arrived. It would all depend on the wind direction, which is determined by how fast the counterclockwise-spinning storm heads north. Thus, the protection of a wet suit is worth the discomfort when water temperatures are unknown.

Geramita explains to the pilots that they need to reposition directly over A.J. so he can be picked up. To save time, the flight mechanic lowers a strop, a big red sling, rather than the hook, to extract the swimmer from the water. Within seconds, A.J. is back in the helo. But a total of five precious minutes has been wasted in this first effort, and there are now only twenty minutes left to bingo time.

Bader and Andry are worried about the mainmast on the sailboat. Including the mast, the *Almeisan* rises fifty-three feet above the waterline. Couple that with a forty-foot wave, and the *Almeisan*'s mast would extend ninety-three feet above the trough of a wave. The pilots need to establish a hover low enough to perform the rescue but high enough so the aircraft will not come in contact with the sailboat. To make matters worse, the mast is wailing back and forth as waves rock the boat. In calmer weather the pilots might hover using the helicopter's "altitude hold" function, but in these seas that would automatically have the Jayhawk bounding up and down thirty or forty feet with each passing wave. The pilots want flexibility in controlling their altitude and they know that the hoist operator requires as much stability as possible, a difficult challenge when the helicopter is being buffeted by gale-force winds. They decide to control the helicopter's altitude manually, staying about fifty to seventy-five feet above the ocean, and higher when near the sailboat.

A.J. and Geramita quickly agree on a new course of action. They tell Andry that they want him to radio the *Almeisan* and have the first survivor jump off the back of the boat, explaining that A.J. will then be lowered as close as possible.

Kathy doesn't hesitate when she hears the instructions. She climbs up the companionway, peeks up at the helicopter, then carefully exits the cockpit and in a crouching walk moves to the stern. The downdrafts from the helicopter's rotors have the surface of the sea boiling in a swirling froth of foam and spray. She takes a last look toward the open door of the helicopter, sees Geramita motioning her to jump, and over she goes.

A.J. is immediately lowered. As soon as he hits the water he unclips from the cable, and using four quick strokes is next to Kathy, holding onto her PFD. He asks her if she has any medical problems, then starts to explain what they are about to do. Neither A.J. nor

Kathy hears or sees a particularly large wave bearing down on them. A.J. rides up the wave face higher than Kathy, and he feels her being pulled from him. He manages to get both hands on her PDF just as the wave avalanches onto their heads. The wave pounds them like a pile driver, and A.J. has only one thought, *Don't lose hold of her.* When the churning stops and they kick to the surface, A.J. is surprised to see that Kathy is composed, saying, "I'm OK. I'm OK."

Meanwhile, Geramita has retrieved the cable, fastened a rescue basket to the end, and begins to lower it. At this point neither of the pilots can see the two people in the water below them, and they must rely on Geramita's instructions for positioning the aircraft. In normal conditions the hoist operator might be giving the pilots instructions to move five or ten feet one way or another. But with the huge seas, the people in the water are drifting quickly while the helicopter is being battered out of position by the wind, and Geramita's instructions are as follows: "Forward and right fifty feet. Now left twenty feet." It takes a couple of minutes to get into position, and the pilots are carefully adjusting their altitude to keep them close but out of range of the waves. When the helo is in the correct position, Geramita informs the pilots. "OK, hold it as best you can. I'm lowering the basket."

When the basket reaches the water, A.J. grabs hold of it and helps Kathy crawl onto it, just as another wave pours over them. The instant the wave passes, A.J. signals to Geramita to retrieve the basket. Nothing happens. A.J. is outside the basket holding on, and again he gives the thumbs-up sign to his hoist operator. Another wave crashes on them and both survivor and rescue swimmer feel like a punching bag for the waves. Kathy is not aware that anything is amiss. All her attention and strength are focused on keeping herself inside the basket. But A.J., with his years of training, knows this isn't in the script, and that something is terribly wrong.

Inside the helicopter's cabin, Geramita has his hands full. The first wave that hit the basket propelled it upward, causing slack in the cable. The thin steel line was then blown backward a few feet, becoming wedged between the helicopter's door and extra fuel tank. Geramita tries pushing the door, then pulling on the cable, but it remains jammed.

Pilots Andry and Bader know something is wrong. They let a few seconds go by and then Bader says, as calmly as possible, "Is everything OK back there?" The commander senses how tense the situation is and doesn't want to add to the pressure Geramita is under.

"The cable is jammed," says Geramita, catching his breath. "It's between the door and the fuel tank. I'm working on it."

There is silence on the headsets now. Andry's mind, however, is racing. *Well, this is great. When we arrived there were three people in a beat-up sailboat and four of us in the helicopter. And now we have a survivor and our rescue swimmer stuck in the ocean whom we can't pull up. If we have to leave the scene there's no way they can get back to the sailboat.*

Andry is dividing his attention between looking out the front of the helo, watching for large waves, and glancing behind him at Geramita so he can advise Lieutenant Commander Bader—who is controlling the aircraft—what is happening. Bader is keeping his focus down and to the right, on the sailboat, using it to help him maintain a stable hover at about seventy feet. The waves are coming in sets of three. Just as Andry and Bader are getting accustomed to the timing and size of the seas, one especially large wave comes barreling toward them.

Andry shouts, "Big wave coming!"

Bader powers the helo into a quick climb. The two pilots look at each other and shake their heads in astonishment.

Andry glances back at Geramita and sees that the hoist operator is now literally hanging outside the doorway, trying to reach farther back on the cable, and he's wearing a "gunner's belt," a belt-like apparatus connected to a strap that is attached to the aircraft.

The copilot holds his breath. He can see the cable from the hoist going toward the tail rotor, where it angles down to the basket being socked by the seas. A survivor is in the basket, A.J. alongside, and it looks as if both are spending as much time under the foam and water as on the surface. A wave pushes the basket from Andry's side of the helo toward Bader's side and he loses sight of it altogether. For a moment the copilot feels time stand still. "Can you see them?" he asks Bader.

The commander answers that he can, but Andry is now speculating about different outcomes, and most of them are not good. If

Geramita cannot free the cable they will have to cut it, leaving the survivor and A.J. in the sea. The hoist operator would then have to determine if there were enough time to do a quick splice and attach a new hook. Andry doesn't think so. The aircraft is also fitted with an emergency rescue device that is basically a rope and a hand crank. The rope can be run through the hoist, but it still must be manually cranked, an incredibly difficult and strenuous process. Andry knows this won't work either, because even in optimal conditions hand cranking just forty feet of line would take half an hour, and with their fuel situation that is simply too long.

CHAPTER TWENTY-FIVE

AN ARMFUL OF TORQUE

Chris is in the cockpit watching Kathy in the rescue basket. He has a feeling of dread. At least four waves have pounded Kathy and the rescue swimmer, and the basket still hasn't been hoisted. He can't help but notice that the sky has darkened, and he figures that in about thirty minutes there will be no light at all. The sailboat is fast drifting away from the helicopter.

Chris glances up at the helo, and through the gloom it looks as if one of the Coast Guardsmen is actually hanging out of the open doorway.

Geramita has one hand on the helicopter frame as the other reaches back in an attempt to grip the cable from a different angle than he did a few seconds earlier. His fingers tighten on the cable and he yanks, then he tries shaking it, but nothing happens. *Damn!* he mutters.

Adrenaline is coursing through him and he's furious. He grabs the sliding door, which is stuck in the open position because of the wedged cable, and yanks with all his might.

The cable pops free. Geramita gives it a quick look to see if there are any overt signs of fraying. The only thing worse than having people in the water is having them fall one hundred feet. The cable looks fine. He knows Bader and Andry are on pins and needles, and Geramita speaks through his headset, trying to steady his voice. "OK, the cable is free. It looks good. I'm retrieving the survivor."

The basket, with Kathy inside, is first dragged across the ocean a few feet, then it is airborne, and finally at the door of the helo. Geramita pulls the basket inside the doorway and helps Kathy crawl out.

"The survivor is in the cabin," says the young hoist operator, unclipping the basket from the hook. "I'm going to bring A.J. up now."

For Andry, copiloting behind a myriad of tiny, brightly colored control lights, the feeling of time standing still is replaced by a sensation that they are in fast forward, harried and rushed. The clock is ticking. The men have only eight minutes to get both Chris and Ron off the boat and into the helicopter. Andry is now updating the crew on the time left, and simply says, "Eight minutes." The wind has blown the sailboat at least three hundred yards away.

Once A.J. is safely inside the cabin, the entire crew confers.

"We gotta do this quicker!" says Bader.

"Forget the basket!" shouts A.J.

The others agree that the basket is too time-consuming. Instead they decide to use a tactic officially called a Strop Augmented Double Pick-Up. None of the men in the helicopter, however, call it that, using instead the old terms "strop" or "horse collar." Whatever it's called, it means that A.J. and the survivor will be hoisted from the ocean together. The strop is nothing more than a sling that hangs from the cable's hook, ready to be looped underneath the survivor's arms. A.J. will also be attached to the hook but by his harness rather than the strop. This type of lift is not as safe as the basket but it's a whole lot quicker.

With Geramita's guidance, Bader and Andry reposition the helicopter above the *Almeisan*. Andry radios Ron and says, "Have the next person come on deck. We'll lower the rescue swimmer and when he motions that person should jump in."

Ron says to Chris, "Good luck, I'll see you up there."

Chris nods. "Right, see you in the helicopter."

Bader and Andry are following Geramita's advice for positioning to keep up with the fast-moving sailboat, when suddenly a fifty-foot wave slams the *Almeisan,* shooting it up toward the aircraft. The mast is heading right toward the helicopter's chin bubble. Bader sees it coming and pulls an armful of torque.

Andry, who does not see the mast, certainly feels the helicopter lurch upward, and shouts, "Whoa, whoa, whoa!" The altimeter shoots from just five feet above the wave to 120 feet as the mountain of water thunders by.

"It's OK!" shouts Bader, "I had to do that. The boat's mast was coming right at us."

The pilots lower the aircraft once again, staying at a cautious one hundred feet above the troughs. "Five minutes," warns Andry.

"I'm lowering A.J.," says Geramita.

Chris is holding onto the lifeline at the stern, watching the helicopter rise and fall with almost as much abruptness as the *Almeisan*. He can see A.J. coming down, spinning in the wind.

The second A.J. hits the water, even before unhooking, he motions for Chris to jump. Chris dives in headfirst and kicks toward the rescue swimmer. He is the only passenger on the *Almeisan* who has not been swept over during the storm, and he's surprised that the water is warm. When he comes to the surface, A.J. is waiting, having unhooked and swum to the survivor. Chris rolls onto his back and A.J. grabs him from behind. For the first time in forty-eight hours Chris relaxes. He closes his eyes and tries to let the tension drain—he is now in somebody else's hands, and he just waits for instructions.

Then the hook gives him a glancing blow on the side of his head. He's OK, but he's going to keep his eyes open from now on.

A.J. drapes the strop over Chris, and tells him to put his arms on the outside of the strop and then lower them tight. The strop is now snug against Chris's armpits. Another strap is secured around his chest. To make sure Chris doesn't slip out, A.J. wraps his legs around Chris's arms, pinning them against the strop. He then lifts an arm and gives the thumbs-up sign to Geramita.

This time the hoist responds immediately and the cable begins pulling them upward. A.J. keeps one hand on the back of Chris's head and the other hand extended, ready to fend off the aircraft.

When they reach the doorway, A.J. feels for the handhold on the outside of the doorway, and when he finds it he hangs on tight, twisting so that Chris is closest to the opening.

Geramita first pulls Chris inside and then helps A.J. in.

A.J. is drenched in sweat but doesn't feel the exhaustion. He's working solely on adrenaline.

Andry shouts out, "Three minutes!"

The two pilots are positioning the helicopter above and just off the stern of the *Almeisan*. Everything is rushed. No extra words are said.

"Lowering the swimmer!" shouts Geramita. For the fourth time in the last twenty-five minutes, A.J. is dropped into the maelstrom.

Andry shouts out, "One minute!"

Bader knows they will go past the bingo time. It's all on him. He looks at Andry and nods. He decides to take the risk.

Andry radios Ron. "OK, it's your turn. Go to the stern immediately and jump when the rescue swimmer motions."

It's been approximately fifteen hours since Ron questioned launching the raft and since his subsequent fall into the ocean. Now he's ready to leave, knowing the *Almeisan* will soon sink.

A.J. doesn't even wait to reach the ocean, but signals Ron to jump when he is halfway down. Once in the water, A.J. unclips, swims to Ron, and spins him around so that he is behind the survivor. "I'm going to put the strop around you!" A.J. shouts in Ron's ear. "Keep your arms down or you'll fall back in the water."

Ron is amazed at the power of the rescue swimmer, as A.J. holds onto his PFD with one arm and strokes with the other, dragging Ron through the water toward the hook and strop. When they reach the cable, A.J. uses his free arm to clip his harness to the hook, then throws the strop over Ron. A.J. wraps his legs around Ron's torso and gives the thumbs-up sign, and the cable lifts them from the water.

Ron feels like his back is going to break. He's so battered and bruised from being swept overboard and thrown down in the boat, he feels as if almost every bone and muscle in his body is being crushed or aching with pain. *Just a few more feet,* Ron tells himself, *and this will all be over.*

When they reach the doorway, Geramita pulls him inside, and the first thing Ron sees are big smiles on the faces of Kathy and Chris, who are sitting in jump seats facing the doorway. An unbelievable feeling of relief sweeps over Ron, and he is near tears as Chris and Kathy reach out to him.

The four Coast Guardsmen feel a sense of satisfaction, but only for a moment. They still have a last hurdle to clear. They have calculated their fuel for the flight to Nantucket anticipating winds from the west. But the winds have shifted and are coming out of the north, meaning they will be flying into headwinds, expending more fuel.

Geramita slams the door shut and they turn north. Below, the *Almeisan,* now a ghost ship, is blown out of sight as darkness closes in.

The Helicopter's Flight Path

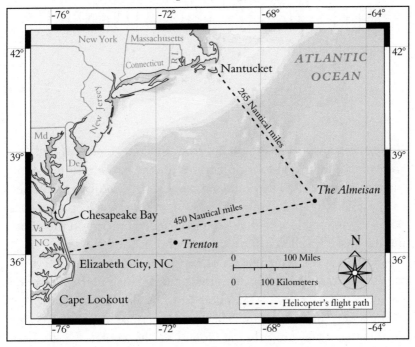

CHAPTER TWENTY-SIX

DARKENING SKIES AND FALLING SPIRITS

Both Andry and Bader, exhausted from the long, tension-filled day, are wearing their night vision goggles for the two-and-a-half-hour flight to Nantucket. The headwinds are strongest at higher altitudes, so the pilots fly at an unusually low two hundred feet above the ocean. Flying so close to the ocean is an added burden on the pilots, but they have no choice due to their fuel situation.

Ahead of them, at an altitude of two thousand feet, a C-130 is acting as escort, resolving all air traffic control issues so the helicopter crew doesn't have to. C-130 pilots Jim Duval and José Zuñiga are in for a very bumpy night. They usually cruise at 250 knots, but on this night they are orbiting around the helicopter at 130 knots. Whenever possible they want to have a visual on the helicopter just in case the chopper goes down. Transponders in the C-130 and in the Jayhawk also allow each aircraft to track the other via radar on a sophisticated electronic system known as TCAS (Traffic Alert and Collision Avoidance System). The C-130 pilots check in by radio with the helicopter pilots every few minutes, making sure they are OK and providing them with weather conditions at different altitudes. Zuñiga is thinking about what a long day it has been, flying to the distress scene, searching for the raft, orbiting the *Almeisan,* and now the nighttime escort mission to Nantucket. The weather at the emergency scene was the worst he has ever been in during his fifteen years of flying for the Coast Guard, and he's not optimistic that anyone could still be alive or found down in the crashing ocean.

When the helicopter launched from the *Trenton* earlier that day, Andry knew they would be pushing their fuel limits, but now he really wonders if they're going to make it. He decides to check his earlier math when he determined the amount of fuel needed to reach Nantucket. This time he adds in the forty-five-knot headwinds they are facing. Assisted by a "whiz wheel" (similar to a slide rule, only round), he recalculates and says to Bader, "It's going to be close. I'm not sure we have enough. . . ."

Bader sighs and smiles. "Don't bother with the calculations, there's nothing we can do now. Either we have enough fuel or we don't."

"You're right," says Andry, putting the whiz wheel back in a cockpit pocket.

There is no in-flight refueling capability from another aircraft. Whatever they have left in their tanks is all the fuel there is.

On the C-130, José Zuñiga, who has been checking on the helicopter's status every ten minutes, breaks in on the radio and says, "Hey, you guys still there?"

"We're here," says Bader.

"OK," says the C-130 pilot, "you were so low you dropped off our TCAS."

Bader says to Andry, "Audie, you know we are only going to have one shot at landing. Our first approach has got to be perfect."

"I know," says Andry. "I was thinking the same thing. You ever land on Nantucket before?"

"No. How about you?"

"Nope. We'll just have to nail it."

Bader thinks about all the times the rescue almost failed, and somehow they solved each hurdle. *Just one more to go.*

In the back of the aircraft, A.J., the thirty-nine-year-old rescue swimmer, has reevaluated each survivor's health, and finds they are all in good shape. Kathy and Chris are sitting on the webbed jump seats on the port side of the aircraft, Ron is on the floor with his back to the pilots, and A.J. and Geramita are sitting aft, facing toward the pilots.

The three survivors are cold, wrapped in blankets, and drinking bottled water. Because of the roar of the whirling rotors, the only way to communicate is to cup one's mouth and move close to the other person's ear. Kathy leans toward A.J. and shouts, "What do you know about the captain and first mate?"

A.J. shouts back, "No news!"

Kathy is certain that Tom and Loch have expired. *Too many hours in the churning ocean, and now it's night. There's no way those men will ever be found.*

A.J. opens his box lunch, offering its contents to the survivors.

Ron shouts, "Am I taking your dinner?"

"No!" hollers A.J. "I don't like to eat while I'm flying!"

The survivors wolf down the sandwiches and think they taste great. This is their first food in over twenty-four hours.

A.J. leans toward Chris, reaches in the survivor's pocket, and pulls out the still-flashing EPIRB.

"Go ahead and deactivate it!" shouts A.J.

Chris had forgotten all about the EPIRB. As he shuts it off, he realizes that without it they would likely be dead. He sits back and closes his eyes, reflecting on everything that has transpired in the last twenty-four hours, thinking how Loch and Tom never really had a chance without the life raft. But the fatigue is too much, and despite sitting up in wet clothes, he falls asleep.

While the helicopter speeds north, Loch is slowly drifting east-southeast as wave after wave continues its assault. As the skies darken, his spirits plummet. He has convinced himself that he will never be found at night, and only in daylight will a ship or plane spot him. But he's having doubts he can hang on until morning. He knows he has weakened even as the seas have grown larger, with a particularly large wave—in excess of thirty-five feet—slamming him every five or ten minutes.

Loch decides to use the last few minutes of dim light to check his gear and move his thoughts off the depressing feeling that he may not outlast the night. He first repositions the two strobe lights so that one is in each pocket of his jacket, then double-checks that his knife is still securely fastened to his harness. Loch wonders about the wisdom of turning on one of the strobes and holding it above his head. On the one hand he is worried about using up the battery power of the strobes when it doesn't seem there are any ships around. And he asks himself how will men in a plane spot a two-inch strobe in the dark if they couldn't see him and Tom in their orange foul-weather gear in the day? Yet, he also remembers how he didn't notice the one ship that did come by him until it was too late. He agonizes over the decision, eventually concluding that from time to time he will take a strobe out, turn it on, and pray for a miracle.

Tom is floating next to him, facedown, but now the deceased man's body is starting to stiffen in the first stage of rigor mortis, with his legs bent at the knee and arms frozen in a position extending beyond his head. Loch is still using Tom for support, and he decides now is the time to reinflate each ditch bag secured to Tom's ankles. Between each wave that breaks on Loch he attends to this chore, telling himself that he and Tom are still a team. *You're helping me stay afloat, and I will bring you back to your family.*

He thinks of Tom as his life raft, but that thought quickly jogs his memory to consider the real life raft and his bold decision to dive inside it in an effort to move it closer to the boat. *Was that the right thing to do?* He replays the series of events leading up to being thrown from the raft, going all the way back to the beginning of the voyage when the captain of a passing sailboat said, "No, *you're* going the wrong way." He remembers the lack of wind and then too much wind, the seasickness, Tom's exhaustion from performing the lion's share of the work, followed by the storm's increasing fury. When the boat rolled completely over he wasn't sure anyone would come out of that alive, and he can still see Kathy overboard shouting, "Help, help!" followed by "Don't let me go!" He recalls going below and seeing the boat in shambles, the broken window, the rising seawater, and the decision to deploy the life raft. *I had to dive into the raft. It might have been our last chance.* He wonders if the *Almeisan* went down, and that brings on a new wave of anguish. Kathy, Ron, and Chris could be at the bottom of the sea, trapped in an overturned boat, or even adrift as he is. He feels the responsibility of their lives weighing on him, and he knows that is further weakening his resolve.

As night settles in, Loch is surprised that although the seas are black, he can still distinguish the horizon, because the sky is a dark shade of gray. Occasionally, through a break in the cloud cover, he can see stars shining through the overcast or even the dim shape of a cloud. He wishes the reverse were true: that he could see the ocean rather than the sky. The waves are so dark he is having difficulty positioning himself so that his back is to the oncoming seas.

The snarling walls of water still drive him down, but now when he surfaces it takes him much longer to orient himself and get prepared for the next one. Every few waves he guesses wrong and takes a blow to the side of his head or directly in the face. He is still trying to scan the seas for a ship sighting, but more of his time is spent preparing for the next wave. Often he is helped by the sky. When he can see a cloud or patch of stars forward of his position he takes a fix on them before being dunked. Then, when he surfaces, he immediately looks for them again and tries to resume the same orientation, so that his back is to the waves.

Still early in the evening a towering wave—unlike any other yet encountered—begins to slide under Loch and he rides higher and higher toward its crest, wondering how much farther he can possibly go. This liquid mountain is so huge he is looking down at the waves to his front and sides, and still he's lifted upward. When he thinks he's near the summit he dares to look behind him and to his right, terrified to see what appears to be an extension of the wave crest, angry, white and foaming. The wind-raked crest looks like a white mane on a black horse, and Loch braces himself to be swallowed by this mass of energy.

Amazingly, his dunking is less severe than from some of the prior waves, and Loch speculates he had just ridden up two waves joined together but with dual crests. Whatever the reason, he is spared what could have been his end. Had the monstrous wave avalanched directly on him, its force would have driven him so deep that he and Tom's body would have tumbled through the vortex longer than he could hold his breath.

The close call leaves him shaken and unnerved. Equally upsetting, he feels that his strength is only about half what it was when he first entered the water. The submersions, the breathing routine, and the constant paddling to keep his back to the seas have him so weary, he's afraid it won't be long before his head will start to hang to the side, just as Tom's did in his final hours. And there's pain too, Loch's arms are sore and feel as heavy as cement, his eyes sting, and his thirst is unlike anything he has ever experienced.

Through his parched lips and cotton mouth he croaks out these words toward the sky: *Just let me hang on until morning.*

CHAPTER TWENTY-SEVEN

NEVER TALK TO THE OCEAN

A.J.'s position in the seat facing the pilots gives him a bird's-eye view of the dashboard. It's approximately 8:15 p.m. and he's been checking the fuel gauge periodically since they left the rescue scene. The gauge is a color-coded bar graph. Green means plenty of fuel and yellow indicates that fuel is getting low. He's watched it go from bright green to bright yellow. This is the first time he has ever seen the bar turn yellow, and it seems like the trip to land is taking forever, as if they are flying in slow motion. A.J. doesn't say anything, not wanting to alarm the survivors, but in some respects this situation is more stressful than being lowered into the thirty- and forty-foot seas. Down in the ocean he had a job to do, a clear focus requiring the maximum out of every muscle and brain cell for decisive action. Now, sitting in the back of the helicopter, he is little more than a passenger. Squinting, he tries to see the bar graph more clearly, but gives up and instead peers out the windows, searching through the fog for lights to indicate that they have reached the island of Nantucket. He sees nothing but black.

Chris has woken up, and he too can see the fuel gauge. When Ron looks at him, Chris rolls his eyes, and Ron's got a pretty good idea that the eye-rolling relates to the fuel situation. Chris considers asking A.J. how far they are from Nantucket, but he sees concern etched in A.J.'s tired face and he decides to remain silent. He forces himself to look away from the dashboard and not think about how the fuel is the only thing keeping this big helicopter from dropping like a stone.

In all their years of flying, Andry and Bader, like A.J., have never seen the fuel gauge go to yellow, but they were expecting this possibility so it doesn't come as a complete surprise. Yet, despite their mental preparation, actually seeing yellow for the first time is more than a little unsettling.

The pilots are as concerned about the fog and heavy rain as they are about the fuel. On their radar they can see the coast of Nantucket and they are matching that to their GPS chart. Then they manually plot a low-level approach path to the airport, clear of any towers, using a paper aviation chart. They are coming in so low that the landing has to be a visual one, even though conditions are well below what is typically required for visual flight rules.

Five minutes later, through the mist and fog, they spot faint lights from Nantucket ahead and below. This is when the fuel caution light starts blinking, indicating they are just about out of fuel. A.J., Geramita, and Chris all see the blinking light as well. A.J. thinks, *Well, at least if we have to put her down suddenly we can do it on land. We might have a chance.* He knows that if they went down in the ocean it would be all over—helicopters are top-heavy because of the rotors and if the aircraft hits the water it's immediately going to roll upside down.

Soon they see the airport with all its runway lights aglow. Andry and Bader bring the helicopter in toward the landing strip, just clearing the treetops. They slow down, and the winds buffet the helo about erratically while the pilots fight to steady the chopper. Everyone is holding his breath.

They start to descend.

When Bader feels the aircraft settle on the tarmac, he slumps in his seat—he has never been so relieved in his entire life. His exhaustion, like a dam being breached, sweeps over him, and he feels he could sleep for days right here in his pilot's seat. Andry turns, lifts off his night vision goggles, and gives him a high five, but Bader thinks that his copilot looks like hell, even worse than when he was seasick on the *Trenton.*

In the rear of the aircraft it's the same: relief mixed with fatigue, including a deep desire to be out of the aircraft and in a warm bed. For the three survivors, the sensation of the aircraft resting on the ground feels odd. It is the first time in several days that they've been sitting without violent motion threatening to knock them over. As the engines are shut down, Kathy, Ron, and Chris hug and thank the aircraft crew, knowing that these four Coasties put their lives on the line—and just a little over the line—for their safe return to land.

Loch's fate, like that of his crewmates, is also in the hands of the Coast Guard. It is now approximately 8:30 p.m., and he has been holding a tiny strobe light on top of his head for the last half hour, hoping for a C-130 to swoop by again. It has been several hours since he has seen a plane, and he worries that perhaps the Coast Guard has checked off his area of the ocean as having been searched. He knows the searchers would plot drift patterns, breaking them into grids, and then search those grids thoroughly, but he also remembers the two C-130s that passed directly over his head without seeing him and Tom. He hopes they will search the area again, but he is painfully aware just how insignificant he is in the immensity of the seas crashing around him.

Aside from trying to give Tom his last rites, Loch is not saying traditional prayers, nor is he calling upon a higher power or divine being for help. It's not that he doesn't believe there is something greater than ourselves, because he does, but his belief does not fit neatly into any one religion. He has a feeling that there is something in the universe—perhaps a form of energy—powerful and more complex than any of us can imagine. Loch is not, however, relying on this force to save him. He has the unwavering conviction that he must rely on himself, and if he can stay positive and focused, the Coast Guard will find him. He tells himself over and over that the Coast Guard is doing its job, and that he needs to be ready to do his part when they locate him.

For the last half hour Loch hasn't seen any stars, and he knows that the cloud cover has sealed in tight. At about 9 p.m. it begins to rain with a vengeance. The cold, horizontally driven rain pelts Loch's face so hard it feels like hundreds of needles being stuck into his skin. To make matters worse, he's desperate for even just a few drops of rain to drink, but when he sticks out his tongue he gets a mouthful of sea spray and foam for his efforts. It's maddening to have fresh water falling from the sky and not be able to quench his aching thirst.

Loch doesn't have the strength to hold up the strobe any longer, and between waves he shuts it off, carefully placing it back in his pocket. Again, near the top of a wave, he tilts his head slightly upward, opens his mouth, and once more it is filled with a salty brew of foam and spray. He lowers the hood of his jacket and tries to hold it open to catch the rain, but his arms are so weak and stiff, he can't grasp it for more than a second or two before a wave buries him. He needs a drink of fresh water in the worst way. It's as if the rain and the ocean are taunting him, adding to his misery.

Then something happens that makes Loch think the sea can read his mind, that the sea is a living, breathing being, and a diabolical one at that. A small wavelet slaps his left cheek smartly, with enough force to make him flinch, conspiring with the rain just to plain piss him off. In frustration, Loch sarcastically blurts out, "Oh nice, now you're coming at me from all sides!"

No sooner are the words out of his mouth than another wavelet belts his face from the right side, jerking his head far to the left and into the water.

Loch feels certain that last slap was in direct response to his derisive comment, and he decides not to talk to the ocean again anytime soon.

Throughout the first half of the night, Loch turns the strobe on and off, and does his best to scan the horizon in all directions. He uses different mind-sets to pass the time and forget his body and his pain. He tries to use his family as motivation, telling himself if he does not survive, no one will ever know how hard he and Tom fought the seas or how Tom tried to give Loch his life jacket at the end. And whenever Loch feels overwhelming despair—the kind that makes him think dying will be easier than going on—he reminds himself of his vow to bring Tom's body back to his family. Tom deserves a proper funeral, and his family deserves a chance to say a last good-bye.

Thinking of Tom's family makes him consider the anguish his own loved ones must be enduring as they worry about his fate. He wishes he could speak to them for just one second and stop their concern by telling them the Coast Guard will find him. But now, at 10 at night, with his teeth chattering from the cold, and his mind becoming dull and muddled, he acknowledges that while the Coast

Guard may indeed find him, he will probably be in such a severe hypothermic state he will be as good as dead. Loch worries that soon he won't be able to use his fingers, knowing his body will retreat from hypothermia from the outside in, ceding his extremities to the cold while trying to protect his core, his vital organs. The human body knows that fingers and toes are dispensable, but the internal organs, especially the heart, must be protected at all costs.

For now, his hands can still clutch the strobe light, and this concentration on his fingers makes him look more carefully at the light he grips. The flashes it emits seem to come less frequently, and Loch struggles to think clearly. *Is my mind playing tricks on me, or were the flashes always this far apart?* He holds the strobe back atop his head, trying to time how frequently it flashes by watching its brief bursts of light glint on the water. The flashes are almost a minute apart, and they are now dim. The batteries are failing. After a couple of more minutes the light becomes so weak and so sporadic it's next to useless, so Loch shuts it and places it in a pocket. Then he removes his second and last strobe light. He fastens the thin rope on the strobe around his wrist and clutches it tightly. His indecision returns about whether to turn it on or keep it off until he actually sees or hears a ship or plane.

He knows it has come down to the little things—such as the power left in a two-inch light—that will likely mean the difference between life and death. He decides to keep the strobe turned on most of the time, with only periodic breaks. *What good is trying to save the strobe for any amount of time beyond tonight?* he asks himself. *If I'm not found in the morning there will be no second night.*

His mood seems to rise and fall like the seas surrounding him. One minute he is hopeful and confident about his survival, and the next his exhaustion gets the best of him, causing his hopes to crash like the crests of the breaking waves. He thinks of Tom's words, "It won't be long now," and knows exactly what he meant—that feeling when you know there's not much reserve strength left. If just one monstrous wave avalanches directly on him, he knows his time will be up. His breathing is so labored, so raspy, his arms so sore, his legs almost useless; there will be no way to come back up from a severe dunking with any air, no time to position himself for the next onslaught. He saw it happen to Tom, and he feels he's not far from where his friend was.

He also craves sleep. Incredibly, despite the violence all around him, he fears he might fall asleep, or maybe succumb to a dumb stupor. His body is crying out for rest. To sleep, however—or even to take a break from positioning himself in the waves—means death.

To help rally his spirits, he reminds himself that of all the people he loves, his daughter Ashley, just thirteen years old, is the one who needs him most. She's at an age where a father is so important. He wants to be there to protect her, counsel her, love her, and to do what he must to keep the thoughts of giving up at bay.

Resolving to battle until he hasn't an ounce of energy left, he continues to use one leaden arm to position himself so that his back is to the waves, while the other holds the strobe light atop his head. Over and over he tells himself, *Just make it to morning.* The word *morning* becomes his mantra; that one word helps crowd out the more desperate, flickering thoughts of how easy it would be to just close his eyes and let go.

CHAPTER TWENTY-EIGHT

HALLUCINATIONS

Prolonged sleep deprivation, particularly the severe kind that Loch is experiencing, will affect judgment, cause carelessness, and even induce a person to take unnecessary risks. The actions of a sleep-deprived person are often similar to those of someone who is drunk, and the ramifications can be just as disastrous. Loch has had no sleep since Friday night because of seasickness on Saturday and being pitched into the sea early Sunday morning. No sleep in more than forty hours combined with expending incredible amounts of energy has left him in such an exhausted state that simple maneuvers such as turning away from the oncoming waves are now being performed slowly, and even erratically. Both his body and mind are reaching the breaking point.

Loch's coordination and reasoning skills will slowly decrease the longer he stays awake, but he's facing another issue due to sleep deprivation—hallucinations—which might have graver consequences. Research suggests that as the neurons in the prefrontal cortex of the brain become increasingly stressed from lack of sleep, their functionality is impaired, and the brain produces images that can be at odds with reality. Although a person may see most of his surroundings correctly, imaginary images may be interjected or a real image altered. The person is conscious, but loses the ability to tell the difference between self-generated and real external stimuli.

And there may be another cause for hallucinations: lack of control over a situation. A research study conducted by professors Adam Galinsky and Jennifer Whitson, recently published in the journal *Science,* illustrates how "participants who lacked control were more likely to perceive a variety of illusory patterns." They explain that the cause of seeing images where none exist is a human's need for structure and direction in chaotic situations.

Loch is certainly in a chaotic situation with little control. Adding to the mix of factors wreaking havoc with his reasoning is the onset of hypothermia, which in its early stages also causes confusion and impaired judgment, and in its moderate stages can bring on hallucinations. As the body attempts to conserve heat it constricts the flow of blood, especially to the peripheries, but the blood is also thickening and flowing more slowly to all parts of the body, including the brain. Each individual reacts differently to such stresses, but there are plenty of reports of hypothermic people "seeing things," becoming "giggly," and even feeling so warm that they take off their clothes.

And so Loch is battling hypothermia, an uncontrollable situation, and sleep deprivation. He craves warmth, sleep, fresh water, and an end to the random violence of the storm. Yet his initial hallucination begins not with his immediate desires, such as the vision of a ship, a life raft, a bed, or drinking water, but with a Nautilus weight-training station!

At approximately 11 p.m. he first spots the object floating in the water, but is unable to tell what it is. Swimming with the waves, he paddles forward and is shocked to see a large black and gray piece of training equipment, complete with bars, weights, and several seats at different stations, jutting out at various angles. *What is this doing here? How can it float?* He notices that the seas have calmed and he can no longer hear the shrieking wind. His spirits rise.

When he comes within a couple of feet of the weight station, he realizes he's going to float right into it and worries about being hit or entangled in the equipment. He ducks his head under the water, dragging Tom with him. When he surfaces and looks back up, the station is now behind him, floating off into the darkness. *What's happening?* He knows he is awake, knows what he saw, but also understands that a weight training machine doesn't just come bobbing by on the ocean. *Is this a reminder to try to get in better shape when I get home?* He shakes his head, confused but not alarmed. A part of him is glad for the distraction, whether real or not.

Although Loch is cold, he does not think the hypothermia is so severe that it poses an immediate threat, or that it alone could be causing him to be losing his grip on reality. He is probably right. It's the combination of all the factors sapping his strength that are making him hallucinate.

No sooner has the Nautilus machine disappeared, than another bizarre image comes bobbing into his vision, this one on a parallel track of sea ahead and slightly to the side of him. It is the front porch of a house. The porch has a roof over it and is supported by natural log posts. Three steps lead down from the porch to a granite landing, floating on the surface of the ocean. When Loch cranes his head to see the rest of the house behind the porch and front door, there is none, only black sky. Again the waves and wind have subsided. *I'm seeing things. It's a mirage. Just ignore it, and get ready for more waves.*

But who can ignore something so close, so strange, and potentially offering safety?

The front porch floats closer now, and Loch finds himself involuntarily moving to intercept it. When the landing is only two feet away, Loch talks to himself, out loud. "Don't step on the landing. It is only a hallucination. It could be trouble."

Despite his admonishment he raises his right foot and lifts it to the landing. He steps right through the granite. Nothing further happens. Rather than get mad at himself, Loch laughs at how gullible he's become, how he can't stop himself from stepping on a stone landing that he knows is not real. *At least I'm not chasing after the porch, at least I know it's an illusion.*

The porch sails out of view, and the roar of the ocean returns with renewed fury, as if to remind Loch that he's had a little break and now it's back to the real world, the death trap of the ocean, which is not done with him.

He fights the fatigue and does his best to keep his face pointed away from the oncoming seas. Yet he wonders about the front porch and how vivid it appeared. *Was there a message for me there? Was the porch sent to tell me to do something different?*

Loch worries that the hallucinations indicate he's losing control of consciousness and will fall asleep at any moment. The odd illusions, however, do have a bright side; they take his mind off the cold, divert it from again thinking of sharks, and occupy it so he doesn't dwell on the other potential hazards that could harm him, one of which is a creature called a Portuguese man-of-war. Being in the Gulf Stream, Loch is directly in the path of these surface-dwelling organisms and their trailing, venomous tentacles that can reach lengths of more than forty feet.

A man-of-war is not a jellyfish, although it does resemble one. Instead, this creature is not a single animal, but four different polyps, and this colony is interdependent, joined together to survive. The part of the main body that bobs on the ocean's surface is a gas-filled float, usually translucent blue, riding the Gulf Stream's current or pushed by the wind, since the organism has no means of propulsion. Beneath the float are groups of polyps with coiled tentacles dangling below. The tentacles contain thousands of stinging cells filled with venom, used to paralyze and then capture prey, such as small fish and shrimp. The creature, however, fires off the venom whenever it comes in contact with just about anything, including humans.

Loch's body is protected from the sting of a man-of-war by his foul-weather suit, but his face and hands are exposed. If he is stung, the welts will hurt like hell, feeling as if he has been electrically shocked and then burnt, but the venom will not directly kill him. Still, the sting may indirectly lead to death, because Loch needs functioning hands and fingers to grip the strobe light and hold it on top of his head. And should he have an allergic reaction to the sting, it could induce shock, harming his heart and lungs. Adding to the threat is that if Loch encounters one man-of-war, chances are there will be more in the vicinity, since they often drift in swarms.

For Loch to avoid a man-of-war—and for that matter hypothermia as well as the other threats to his life—there is only one solution: get rescued before it's too late.

While Loch thinks about porch steps, Nautilus equipment, and his need for sleep, he continues to do his best to scan the sea in all directions. Suddenly he glimpses a flicker of movement to his left, and stiffens. Then, directly in front of him, he sees something dart by just an inch or two above the water. He looks upward and sees two shadows hurl by, and now he knows the objects are small birds. He is not certain what kind they are, but on his past trips to Bermuda he has seen them before. The birds are probably storm petrels, pelagic birds that come to land only when breeding.

There are several of these seabirds all around Loch, hovering, soaring, dipping, and gliding as they snatch small crustaceans and fish from the waves. He feels certain they are not an illusion and is heartened to see life of any sort in such a storm. The grace of the birds mesmerizes him and he is so absorbed in watching them that he forgets his pain. One bird hovers directly in front of his head, staring at Loch, perhaps wondering what on earth he is. The bird moves to Loch's right, then to his left, then hovers dead center, just a foot or two from his head, all the while staring at the weary survivor.

"Go find us some help," says Loch.

The bird does not move, so Loch flicks some water at it, and it scoots up and over the oncoming wave crest and vanishes. The other birds do the same.

Loch is left alone with Tom. He rests his head on his dead friend's back, trying to save what little energy he has left. He notices that the flashes on his second strobe light are getting further apart, and knows when its battery dies he will have no light with which to signal.

CHAPTER TWENTY-NINE

STRANGE LIGHTS

In Portsmouth, Virginia, at the Coast Guard Rescue Coordination Center (RCC), no one has ever been involved in a case this complex. Because the weather is so bad, and because the *Almeisan* distress scene is so far from land, the various search and rescue (SAR) controllers have pulled out all the stops, using all available Coast Guard resources. They are also working with the AMVER vessels, which in addition to the *Sakura Express* now include the motor vessels *Front Brabant* and *Castillo de Butrón,* as well as the two Navy ships, the *Seay* and the *Trenton.* The three controllers on duty are either glued to their computer screens, keeping track of resources, developing future plans, and monitoring intricate search models, or they are on the phones that can connect them with air stations and sector offices and even patch them through to the aircraft pilots at the emergency scene. The center has been a hive of energy ever since the *Almeisan*'s EPIRB was activated some twenty hours ago.

To search for Loch and Tom, the SAR team first used a program called the Computer Aided Search Planning model (CASP). The controllers input what is being searched for (i.e., boat or individual in the water) and its last known position. Then the program pulls in the latest weather forecasts for winds and ocean currents. CASP processes the data, indicating which area of the ocean needs to be searched, and which specific section of that area contains the highest probability for success. The controllers then direct the vessels and the aircraft to search different grids, with the highest-probability region receiving the most attention. On paper the patterns look like lined boxes, some of them overlapping. Each box is an area for a specific ship or plane to search, and the boxes are of different sizes, with the C-130s handling larger grids, such as a twenty-mile by twenty-mile patch of ocean, or four hundred square miles. It's a lot of sea to cover when you are looking for a flash from a two-inch strobe.

The controllers have also calculated the two men's survivability time frame, based on information received from logistician Donna Christman, family members, and later from Chris, Kathy, and Ron. Specifics such as a person's age, height, weight, girth, capabilities as a swimmer, and clothing worn at the time of the accident are all input into a survivability model. Besides giving expected survival time for a person in the water, the model also calculates "functional time," indicating how long a survivor can still help himself by doing such things as activating a strobe light or lighting a flare. The model has shown that by late Sunday evening, Loch and Tom should be well beyond functional time, and are in the stage where death is expected. But SAR coordinators also know that certain people defy the statistics—sometimes through luck but more often because of a will to live—and the search team is hoping the missing men fall into this category.

The SAR supervisor, Geoffrey Pagels, had been off duty that Sunday, but because of the difficulties of the case, he was receiving regular updates at his home and providing guidance to the team on duty. He was well aware of how challenging it would be to find the two missing men.

On Monday morning at 4:30 a.m., he arrives at the Rescue Coordination Center, after a mostly sleepless night thinking about this search and rescue case. He reviews the planned efforts, and knows that first light on scene is crucial because the survivability model doesn't offer much hope beyond that.

At approximately 3 a.m. Loch wonders if the storm has stalled directly above him, because there has been no abatement in the height of the waves or power of the wind. Sometimes a low-pressure system bumps up against a high-pressure system, and they battle for position, causing the storm to wobble or simply stop its forward progression. The storm Loch is in does neither, and it slowly proceeds to the north. It is such a large low-pressure system, however, that he is still within its clutches almost two full days after it first hit the *Almeisan,* blew out the plastic windows in the pilothouse, and breached a porthole in the cabin.

Loch is doing everything in his power to stay awake, positive, and active. He's afraid that if he stops thinking, positioning himself, and scanning the horizon for searchers, the Coast Guard will eventually find two lifeless bodies.

As if to help keep him alert, the surface of the sea fills with a luminescent light, glowing brighter whenever a wave breaks. Loch stares in awe. He observes that even Tom, temporarily trapping water in the seams of his foul-weather gear, glows briefly as a wave washes over him.

The eerie light is a result of a natural phenomenon from living bioluminescent plankton, organisms undergoing chemical reactions that brightly shimmer on the ocean's surface. This event is often referred to as phosphorescence, because when it was first studied, the light was mistakenly assumed to be caused by phosphorus. Writers from Hemingway to Steinbeck have described the glowing ocean, as did Jules Verne in *20,000 Leagues Under the Sea.* Verne mentions the unusual light in conjunction with the Gulf Stream on the exact same day of the month that Loch's ordeal began, writing, "I must add that, during the night, the phosphorescent waters of the Gulf Stream rivaled the electric power of our watch-light, especially in the stormy weather that threatened us so frequently. May 8th we were still crossing Cape Hatteras. . . ."

Loch isn't sure what's causing the shimmering light, but he is grateful for its beauty. Somehow he doesn't feel quite so alone. Even his salt-sore eyes don't seem to sting as much. When he is propelled near the top of a wave, the scene looking down is akin to that of peering out an airplane's window, with lights of towns glowing and lots of darkness in between. As with his earlier hallucinations and the visit of the storm petrels, for a moment he forgets his dire predicament and just enjoys the show.

Then he hears a loud rumbling noise, which turns into a roar. Looking up, he sees a large plane coming from behind his right shoulder, moving forward, then past him. The plane is low enough that Loch sees its two wingtip lights flashing.

Loch waves his minuscule strobe light furiously. The plane

climbs a bit and then banks to the left, but continues to fly away from him.

A wave tumbles down on Loch, dragging him and Tom underneath its foaming crest. When Loch struggles back to the surface, the plane is gone.

Could that have been a hallucination? Loch isn't sure. It seemed so real, so clear, and in such detail. Yet it was extremely brief, appearing for only three or four seconds. He eventually decides the plane is real. *Hang on a little longer. They're still searching for us.*

He goes back to being mesmerized by the bioluminescence around him, particularly as it runs off the back of Tom's foulweather gear. *It must be getting near morning.* His thoughts go in all different directions, and he's riding the waves as if on automatic pilot, so exhausted he's not sure if he's even fully conscious. A few minutes later disaster strikes.

A particularly large wave hammers into Loch, striking him from the front, forcing the air out of his lungs and driving his head backward, filling his nose with water. Then the wave rams him and Tom below. Caught off guard, Loch makes the mistake of trying to get air. He ingests a considerable amount of water, and is now coughing and gagging, still under water. It seems an eternity that the wave holds him below, pinning him in its belly. Water swirls around him in all directions, and Loch isn't sure which way is up, but he can't wait for his PFD to pull him to the surface; he feels he might pass out at any second. Instinct takes over in his fight, and he's kicking with his legs and pulling with his leaden arms, like a boxer trying to take some last shots even as he's careening to the canvas.

He pops to the surface and lets out a loud gasp, followed by hacking and spitting up water.

For the last twenty-four hours he has relied on his breathing pattern, along with keeping his back to the waves, for survival, and this is his first major failure. As he slowly recovers and gets ready for the next wave he thinks, *Is this the end? This is how Tom was at the end.*

But, as in the past, just the thought of Tom gives him a nudge, a bit of focus. *You've come this far. You promised to get Tom home.*

The waves return to normal size, and Loch continues his routine of holding his breath before they break on him, letting his PFD bring him back up, then orienting himself for the next one. And between hits he's got time to think. He goes back to the world of luminescent light around him, losing himself in its glow, letting time pass.

One point of light on his forearm does not seem to be moving, and he concentrates on its dim glow. It appears, disappears, and reappears in the exact same spot. *That's strange, all the other light drains back into the water. Why not this one?*

A wave propels him upward, and now he realizes this one point of light is not on his arm, but is actually far away on the seas. In Loch's confused state it takes him a couple of minutes to understand what he is looking at. Then it hits him. *A ship! The tiny glow is a range light on the top of a ship!*

CHAPTER THIRTY

THE WEAKENING STROBE

Loch doesn't know it, but the C-130 that flew close to him, and that launched from Clearwater, Florida, did indeed spot his strobe light, if only for a second. Pilots Mark Russell and Ben Maitre were flying the aircraft at an altitude of about four hundred feet when Maitre thought he saw a dull flicker of light and shouted out, "Mark! Mark! Mark! Two hundred yards off the right wing!" He wasn't hollering at his fellow pilot; instead he was alerting the flight navigator in the cabin of the plane to mark this spot on his control panel because Maitre had seen a light. He was surprised by the sighting; anytime a person is in the water far from shore it's a long shot they will be seen, especially at night.

Also on the plane's flight deck were a flight engineer and navigator, and back in the cargo compartment were two drop masters, who also tried to spot the strobe. The drop masters were sitting above two twenty-inch rectangular windows specially erected near the bottom of the aircraft, allowing each a view of the ocean below. But the plane had moved past the strobe, and no one besides Ben Maitre saw it.

Maitre, actually an Air Force pilot participating in an exchange program with the Coast Guard, wondered if he really did see a strobe. *Could it have been something else?* he asked himself. But when the plane circled back for another look, again Ben glimpsed a dim light, and shouted, "Mark! Mark! Mark!" No one else on the aircraft spotted the light, yet Maitre was convinced something was down there.

They banked hard to the left to give a visual mark for the crew of the *Sakura Express* so they could see the area where the pilot spotted the light. Pilots Russell and Maitre immediately tried to vector in the *Seay* and the *Sakura Express* by radio but were unable to do so,

165

and instead told Portsmouth of their sighting and the position. They reported that they had seen what they believed to be a strobe, but that it was too dark to see if there was a survivor with the light.

Portsmouth relayed the information to the *Seay*: "CG1717 (C-130) unable to contact you. Requested to pass that they are OK. They have spotted a strobe in position 37–38.4n 066–40.6w. CG1717 have requested that *Seay* direct one of the vessels to the position to investigate. Will recalculate the drift and send you some patterns for the vessels."

A few minutes later Portsmouth updated the C-130: "One of the vessels is en route to the strobe. . . . FYI, just got info from the debrief [of Chris, Ron, and Kathy] and understand that their PFD's do have strobes."

The C-130 orbited the area where the strobe was seen, and after a few minutes of searching, Maitre thought he saw it again, but the light was fainter than before. He radioed a Canadian C-130, which also recently had arrived on scene, and alerted them to the sighting.

Maitre noticed the *Sakura Express* heading to where he saw the light, but he wasn't at all confident that the crew on such a large ship would be able to locate the dim strobe.

Seeing the ship should be cause for hope, but his hallucinations have made Loch worried and confused. Ahead of the ship Loch sees a large island covered with palm trees. He wonders what's real and what's imaginary. Even worse, it appears that if the vessel stays on its present course, it will pass behind the island and obstruct the view of those on board who might be searching for him.

Frantically, Loch holds his strobe as high as possible and waves his arm so that the weakening flashes of light are aimed toward the ship.

The ship is close enough now that Loch can see a green starboard running light, a forward range light, and the original range light near the stern of the ship. It continues plowing through the mountainous seas, heading toward the island. Loch shouts at the ship but realizes he is much too far for anyone to hear him. The strobe is his only chance.

If this is all hallucinations, I'm finished. Every time a wave buries Loch he comes up fearing the ship and island might be gone, and he doesn't think he can take such a setback. But the ship is still there and so is the island.

Then the lights on the ship change position and start to align in a row. It now appears that the ship is coming toward Loch and will not pass behind the island. The island vanishes, and Loch concludes it was a hallucination but that the ship is real because it remains, slowly heading in his direction.

The optimism this gives him is tempered by the dimming flash of the strobe, which he can no longer hold high above the water. He lowers his weary arm and presses the strobe against his forehead, with its reducing light aimed toward the ship. He hears the C-130 passing from his left to right somewhere in front of him, but with the waves and air-blown foam, he cannot see it.

Loch's neck muscles are so fatigued that he can no longer keep his head held high, and it hangs to the side, chafing against his PFD. A wave plunges him and Tom under its breaking crest, and Loch has difficulty holding his breath. When his PFD pulls him to the surface he's disoriented, desperately trying to locate the ship. Instead he sees a large light in the water that he thinks was dropped earlier from the C-130. He concludes the ship is somewhere behind the light. He starts swimming to the light, dragging Tom's body behind him, hoping that once at the light the ship's crew will easily find him. The light is enormous, however, elevated on a platform, and he wonders how the C-130 ever managed to drop it in the ocean. He doesn't dwell on the thought but instead focuses on his objective: make it to the light before his strobe goes dead. And once at the light, he will clip his and Tom's tether to it and wait there, even if he's got to hang on until dawn.

Suddenly from out of the coal black sky zooms the C-130, passing directly over Loch. The plane is so low he can briefly feel the air swirl around him. He waves his yellow bag and manages to crisscross his arms above his head before the plane roars out of sight. He feels certain that the plane has seen him. But where is the ship?

Loch continues to dog-paddle toward the light, sometimes dragging, sometimes pushing Tom's body. Another wave engulfs him. This time when he surfaces and sees the light he is taken aback by how high up it is. The light is enormous and seems to be increasing in size. Then, in a flash of clear thinking, he realizes that this glowing light was not dropped from the C-130, is not on a tower, and is not a signal light at all. It is the light on the bow of the ship, and it is bearing directly down on him.

Grabbing Tom's PFD collar, Loch madly swims toward the left to avoid getting run down. He tries to keep Tom close to him. The ship is so close that he fears that if he drags Tom on his tether, the ship's bow might split them apart or drag them under.

On board the *Sakura Express,* one of the crewmembers gets a brief look at the faint blink of the strobe. From high up on the ship's deck, the strobe looks to be floating in the water, not attached to any PFD or person. Again the crewmember sees the weak light, and again the strobe seems to be bobbing alone in the ocean. Because the seas are so large it appears as if the strobe is skimming across the water and no one could possibly be attached to it. But in a sea state like this, the ocean can play optical tricks, making it look like the strobe—which is now only giving a sporadic dim blink—is racing along, when in fact much of the movement is the ocean rushing by.

The *Sakura Express* radios the Navy ship *Seay,* which in turn notifies Portsmouth, saying: "The *Sakura Express* is on-scene with the strobe. All they report is a strobe, no PFD or anything else attached to it. What would you like them to do?"

Portsmouth responds: "Have them search that area with the strobe as the center point."

At Portsmouth, the elation felt earlier by the SAR coordinators when the strobe was first located is replaced by more anxiety. They know that survival time for anyone in the water is about over. However, they also conclude that the ship's crewmember who first saw the strobe is likely mistaken, and the strobe must be attached to a PFD, if not a body.

The coordinators put the strobe news behind them, refocus on the task at hand, and slightly revise the search patterns for the AMVER vessels. The exhausted coordinators are coming to the realization that unless they get a break, their search and rescue will become search and recovery.

Of course Loch is unaware that anyone on the ship has seen his strobe—he's too busy trying not to be run down by 30,000 tons of steel. He's got a grip on Tom's PFD with one hand and is using the other, as well as his legs, to propel himself away from the looming hull.

Just as he makes it to the starboard side of the *Sakura Express* and beyond the reach of the approaching bow, Loch realizes his strobe has gone completely dead. He continues to paddle a few more feet away from the ship's hull, and in the process the strobe slips off his wrist and is lost. Overhead, the Canadian C-130 is dropping parachute flares, hoping to illuminate the area so that the *Sakura* crew can spot Loch.

Out of breath, Loch feels that his pounding heart is ready to burst. He floats, wheezing and gasping for air. Through the gloom, he looks up at the ship whenever it is partially illuminated by a flare. The vessel is enormous, almost six hundred feet in length, and its hull is orange. It is moving very slowly. When a wave propels Loch upward he is almost as high as the ship's deck, and he shouts and tries to wave his leaden arms. There doesn't appear to be anyone on the deck, but the deck lights are on.

The ship is inching past him. *I'm so close, they've just got to see me.*

He glances to the east, hoping to see a faint bit of light, but the sky is black. Already he is preparing himself for the worst, preparing himself to try to stay afloat another hour and hope a helicopter can search low enough and slowly enough to find him.

Despite the anguish of not being seen and having help just a few feet away, his resolve is still strong, considering the setback. But his body is not. It's hard for him to keep his head straight, hard to keep from ingesting seawater. And so he rests, trying to conserve what's left of his energy.

Suddenly, the sea, just forward of Loch, is illuminated by a piercing light. From high up on the ship's superstructure the vessel's searchlight is making a slow sweep toward Loch. He yells for all he's worth, and again tries to raise his arms. The light passes directly over his head, continues toward the stern of the ship, and comes back around, shining a bit farther out. Then the light abruptly goes out.

Again Loch thinks how close he is to rescue but no one can see him in the foaming seas. The frustration he feels is heartbreaking. The ship continues to inch past him.

Whatever inner will is driving Loch to keep going reasserts itself and fuels a bit of newfound energy. Perhaps in an effort to keep his sanity, he compels himself to at least achieve one little goal. He decides that no matter what happens he simply has to know the name of this ship. The objective gives him something to focus on, something within his control. He is not going to let the ship slip into the night without at least learning its name. He may die, but he feels a sense of gratitude for the men on the vessel who are trying to find him.

As the ship wallows in the thirty- and forty-foot seas, Loch struggles to stay near it, anticipating that he will be directly behind the stern of the vessel in a minute or two. He notices a discharge pouring from a large-diameter pipe, but has no idea what is being released. When the stern is abreast of him he listens for the sound of propellers and tries to see if the water is churning from turning propellers. He neither hears nor sees any sign that the propellers are in use, and he risks swimming closer to the vessel. But despite being just a few feet away from the flat stern, he cannot see any lettering in the darkness.

The effort is not totally wasted, however, because as Loch kicks to the port side of the stern, he notices the seas on this side of the ship are considerably lower than they were on the starboard side. The *Sakura Express* is so massive it's providing a lee from the wind and waves.

Unbeknownst to Loch, crewmembers were on the deck of the *Sakura Express,* and they *did* see a weak strobe flash when Loch first swam clear of the bow. That was why the searchlight came on. As the searchlight scanned the ocean, some of the crew erupted in shouts—for a split second they saw a person in the water, not far from the ship's hull.

Sakura Express's Captain Tolja radioed the Navy ship *Seay,* which relayed the message to Portsmouth: "*Sakura Express* reports they have a PIW [person in water] in position 37–38.2n 066 46.3w. Unsure of status of PIW."

Portsmouth reiterated this news for all to hear, followed by their concern that the C-130s had enough fuel to remain on scene until the PIW was rescued: "*Sakura Express* has spotted a PIW. Not sure if he's alive or not. Please ask CG1717 how much time they have O/S [on scene] and also have them reach out to the Rescue 328 [Canadian C-130] and find out how much time they have O/S."

A couple of minutes later crewmembers on the *Sakura* heard a shout from the seas below and they hollered back in return. They were unable to get a glimpse of the survivor, but now they knew he was alive.

Captain Tolja radioed the *Seay,* and that ship passed the following message to Portsmouth: "Confirmed that the one PIW is alive. Vessel [*Sakura*] is alongside and attempting to pick him up. Having a rough time due to weather."

Then the survivor was gone from the view of those on the *Sakura Express.* Even with the searchlight making another sweep, the survivor seemingly vanished. Captain Srdan Tolja completely stopped the ship's forward movement, and all hands on deck listened for another shout from the darkness. All they could hear was the blasting wind and crashing seas.

The *Seay* relayed the bad news to Portsmouth: "The Sakura Express has been unable to pick up the PIW and has lost sight of him. Both birds are above the position searching. Ceiling at six hundred feet."

Captain Tolja ordered smoke signals to be deployed in the area where the survivor was seen, and he also helped mark the spot by discharging oil from a pipe. He radioed the C-130 pilots, informing them that he had marked the area where the survivor was spotted with smoke signals and oil. He asked the Canadian C-130 to cease dropping flares. Then the captain ordered the searchlight extinguished in hopes his crew can once again see the flash of the survivor's strobe light.

Now no one on board the ship knows that the flash they saw earlier was the very last one from the strobe before it died.

CHAPTER THIRTY-ONE

ONE LAST SHOUT

Captain Tolja's mind is racing. He's had smoke signals dropped and oil discharged, and has even thrown life rings overboard, yet he's wondering what more he can be doing. He has stopped the *Sakura Express,* knowing that the man in the water is close by, and he does not want the ship to injure him. He also orders all deck lights turned off to aid in the night vision of his crew searching the hilly seas. His men strain to see a flicker of light or hear a muffled cry.

Tolja also considers the emotions of the man in the water and thinks that if the survivor can see that the ship is not moving, it will help his morale, give him determination to hang on a bit longer.

In the lee of the port side of the ship, Loch is able to push Tom's body ahead of him and kick toward the bow. Every couple of minutes he rests, and shouts as loud as he can.

"Help, Captain, over here!"

Loch realizes he's yelling into the wind and assumes the sound of his voice is simply swept back away from the ship. He starts to formulate a plan. *Get upwind of the ship so they can hear me. This might be my last chance.*

Approximately forty-five minutes have gone by with Loch swimming alongside the ship, but time means nothing to the heaving seas; Loch's fate is still in the hands of the ocean. Even on the protected side of the ship, he's got to be careful of the enormous orange hull, which is almost the length of two football fields. Whenever a wave sends the hull upward, a vacuum is created alongside it, and water races in to fill the void. Then when the hull crashes back down, it sends out its own swirling whirlpools of water. Amazingly, despite hypothermia, dehydration, and sleep deprivation, Loch is aware of all the dangers around him. He constantly makes sure there are at least fifty feet between him and the hull.

He continues pushing Tom, kicking, resting, and yelling, all the while advancing toward the bow. He wonders how, in such huge seas, the ship seems to be able to stay in one place. On the outside of the vessel's hull, not far from the deck, Loch spots a gangway in the horizontal position. For a moment he pauses below it and waits for a wave to carry him up toward its rail, thinking that he can grab onto it and maybe his cries will be heard. The waves, however, are too violent, and Loch realizes he'll be crushed to death against the steel gangway and hull long before he can get a handhold. He resumes moving toward the bow, certain that getting upwind is his only chance.

Foot by foot he shoves Tom forward along the port side, and soon he is at the bow. He has now made a complete circle around the huge ship, and realizes the best place to be heard will be on the starboard side of the bow. To get there he starts kicking across the front of the bow. But he pauses halfway across, hearing a strange mechanical noise. The low rumbling sound sends a wave of fear shooting up Loch's spine.

Loch thinks he now knows how the ship is able to hold position. It might have bow thrusters—propellers mounted in the front of the ship to help it maneuver. These propellers are housed at either end of a tunnel going right through the bow of a ship, below the waterline. One propeller is on the port side of the bow and the other on the starboard side. They allow the captain to rotate the vessel slowly even when the main propulsion mechanism is not operating, thus allowing turns without forward motion. They can also be used to hold position in heavy seas.

Loch can't be sure, but he believes the propellers are whirling and churning just a few feet away. He is kicking as hard as he can, terrified of being sucked into the vortex created by the propellers. He's no longer even thinking of rescue—now all he wants to do is put some distance between him and the steel blades.

He makes it 100 yards from the starboard side of the bow and stops, completely spent, unable to lift his arms, kick, or even raise his head. He simply floats.

The ship's deck lights are back on and the Canadian C-130 has gotten the OK to resume dropping flares, and down they float. Loch watches as one just misses landing on the deck, and he worries that if a flare lands in the wrong spot the whole ship could explode. He has no idea that the *Sakura Express* is loaded with jet fuel, but he's hoping it's carrying a cargo of cement!

Quickly, however, Loch considers the flares as an opportunity. He reaches in his bug-out bag and removes a three- by four-inch piece of polished metal designed to be used as a reflective mirror. Holding it high above his head, angling it toward a nearby flare, he hopes the metal picks up the reflection of the light. This takes a tremendous amount of effort as he kicks and twists his body to keep the metal aimed at the descending light of the flare. Then the flare is swallowed by the sea.

Seeing no reaction on the ship, Loch succumbs to his frustration, and breaks his rule not to talk to the ocean. "Let us go!" he hollers in total despair. "Can't you see they are here to help us? Let us go!"

As soon as his plea is out of his mouth and snatched by the wind, the sea answers him. In quick succession, three enormous waves bury him and Tom, sending them tumbling through the white water and foam. When the last of the waves passes by and Loch struggles to the surface, he is completely disoriented. He cannot even locate the ship. Twice he spins around, now on the verge of panic, but still there is no ship.

Loch is looking for a ship with its deck lights on, but during his dunking by the three large waves, the vessel's lights have gone off again and the Canadian C-130 has stopped dropping flares. Finally Loch sees the dark looming hull of the ship, and it's slowly sliding past him, about 200 yards away. Loch slams his hand on the water, and cries out, "What can happen next?" His thoughts are jumbled and confused, but he does manage to answer his own question: *I could be eaten by a shark.* For only the second time during his ordeal he is bedeviled by the thought of sharks lurking beneath him. He is so consumed with this terror, he actually opens the knife that is attached to his harness.

Just then a furious sea catches him and Tom, plunging them head over heels. When Loch regains the surface he realizes he's lucky he didn't slash himself with the open knife. With trembling fingers he struggles to close it, finally succeeding in getting the blade back into the slot. *If a shark comes I'll just have to reopen it. But nothing would be worse than having the ocean stab me with my own knife as we tumble down a wave.*

Loch watches as the ship begins to drift pass him, and because the vessel has turned off its lights he thinks they are giving up the search. It has taken him well over an hour to circle the vessel, and he's no closer to rescue than when he first spotted the tanker. He simply cannot let it leave him. Putting Tom in a perpendicular position in front of him, he starts kicking toward the hull. Once a minute he pauses, rests, and shouts as loud as he can, "Captain, Captain, help!" Still no lights or movement on the ship.

Loch's voice, partially from dehydration and partially from all his prior shouting, is growing weaker, and his yells are sounding more and more like unintelligible croaks. He's got one last idea, and that is to make it to the hull and then bang on it with the metal clip on his harness.

But his progress is slow, and he begins to think that the ship will have drifted past him before he can close the gap. He can't believe that all his struggles during the past twenty-six hours will end in failure, and all within sight of the rescue ship. The heartache of coming so close, only to fail, is almost more than he can take. He continues his weak kicks but feels rescue is slipping away like so much foam on the windswept seas.

Loch's got energy for one last shout, and he lets out a final "Help!"

Suddenly all hell breaks loose on the deck. There is movement, yelling, and the deck lights spring back to life, illuminating the superstructure of the massive tanker.

Loch shouts, "Over here!" Then hollers a question, "Is a helicopter coming?"

"No!" he hears in reply.

Loch kicks as hard as he can toward the hull, and the ship's searchlight finds him. He hears someone ask, "What is your name, who are you?"

Loch wonders why in the world anyone would ask such a question. There can't be anyone else out here in the middle of the ocean! He shouts back, "It's Loch Reidy and Captain Tom Tighe! Tom is dead!"

Loch's mind is racing with all manner of thoughts. Again he considers why the crew should ask who he is, and his only conclusion is that perhaps the rest of the crew from the *Almeisan* ended up in the sea.

In these chaotic conditions Captain Tolja has to be extremely careful as he maneuvers the vessel toward the floating survivor. One ill-timed wave can pick the vessel up and either suck Loch under the ship or slam it right into him. Every bit of the captain's experience and seamanship is summoned forth. He has no idea how much the survivor is going to be able to aid in his own rescue, but Captain Tolja is counting on Loch to be cognizant of what is happening around him and able to react when necessary.

The ship and Loch have closed the gap between them, and one of the crewmen throws out a line with a life ring attached. The wind blows it right back on deck. Next, the crewmember lowers the life ring down the side of the ship and it touches the water near the survivor.

Loch grabs the ring, looping his arm through it. The crewmember starts to pull. A wave washes under Loch and as the cresting wall of water drops from under him, he is left hanging in the air with Tom below him. He loses his grip and falls back into the sea.

CHAPTER THIRTY-TWO

THE CARGO NET

When Loch hits the water he has the breath knocked out of him, and he floats on his back, stunned. He has endured as much as humanly possible and this latest setback chips away at his resolve. *Is each effort eventually going to end in failure? The sea won't let me go.*

The waves send him on a sickening ride alongside the ship. One minute he is in the trough next to the rusted area of the hull, then he rockets upward past the waterline on the ship where the orange paint is clean, and continues rising almost as high as the deck before plunging back down. At the bottom he sees where the hull curves toward the keel and it flashes through his mind that he's going to be caught under the ship and crushed. He tries to kick, but his legs aren't really responding, and it's a struggle to keep clear of the hull. To make matters worse, he and Tom are drifting aft, where the wind will carry his voice away from the vessel and into the void. Loch fears the crew will once again lose sight of him, and no amount of shouting will help.

Then he sees it: a large cargo net being lowered by a deck crane. The net, made of rope, is shaped like a pouch or bag, and is suspended by a cable. It is only ten feet away from Loch, and the sight of it gives him a boost of energy and a real sense of hope. He pushes Tom to the net, unhooks the tether on the harness that has kept him with his friend for so long, and finds an opening in the net. He pushes Tom inside. Then the net starts to rise.

Loch scrambles to grab hold of the outside net with his hands and is also able to get his feet inside the webbing, but his torso is suspended in the air. As it rises the net swings perpendicular to the hull. Loch feels his arms shaking, going numb. "Hurry! Hurry!" he screams.

He looks down toward the black seething sea, and it's at that moment that he sees Tom floating directly below. Tom has fallen out of the net.

Horrified, Loch cannot leave his friend, and he prepares to jump. But his feet are stuck inside the net. Just as he manages to free one foot, the crane swings the net onto the deck.

The crew of the *Sakura Express* is waiting. They remove Loch's feet from the net but insist he lie down. Loch, however, says, "I'm OK, I'm OK." Then he tries to stand and collapses back onto the net.

A stretcher is brought out, and Loch is carefully lifted onto it. Captain Tolja is next to Loch and says, "You kept your captain all this time?"

"Yes," Loch says, "he's dead, but you've got to get him."

"We will, we will. We saw him fall from the net."

The stretcher is now being moved toward some stairs, and Captain Tolja walks alongside. He grips Loch on the shoulder and says, "The others on board the sailboat have all been rescued. They are all OK."

The feeling of relief that sweeps through Loch is so intense it feels like his body is shutting down. He cannot speak. He is barely conscious of his surroundings.

Loch feels himself being carried down two flights of stairs and opens his eyes when they stop in what appears to be a medical room. Helping hands lift Loch from the stretcher and onto a bed. They remove all of his wet clothing and cover him in blankets.

Captain Tolja radios the *Seay,* and they in turn let Portsmouth know the good news. "*Sakura* has recovered one PIW. Reported that Mr. Lochlin Reidy has been recovered alive and is on board. Passed that the captain passed away. He was with him."

In Portsmouth, the SAR controllers cannot believe anyone was found alive. Most thought they might find bodies after dawn but not a survivor, and especially not now. Finding a PIW far out at sea and at night is virtually impossible. The exhausted SAR team is ecstatic and there are high fives all around. They all remember plenty of other SARs where there were no survivors. The news is so unexpected that they even call Libby Pruitt, the SAR controller who had worked the phones for twelve hours and is now home in bed. "Libby," they tell her, "you're not going to believe this, but we got one of the PIWs and he is alive."

Then it's back to business for Portsmouth. They still want to recover Tom, and radio the C-130s and the *Seay*: "We would like for the aircraft to stay O/S along with the *Seay* and *Sakura Express* and search for the captain. The other two AMVER vessels are released."

Back out at sea in the *Sakura's* medical room, Loch is vaguely aware that someone is taking his blood pressure while a thermometer is placed in his mouth.

Loch opens his eyes and sees several people standing around him, all with looks of concern. Except for the captain and the engineer, who are not in the room, the entire crew is Filipino. The handful of crewmembers hovering about are watching every move this miracle man makes.

Loch breaks the silence and asks, "Are there women on board?"

The crew looks at Loch like he has lost his mind. They exchange glances and say, "No, no women." They don't understand that the reason Loch asked the question is because when he was in the water and heard yelling from the ship he thought some of the voices were female, and was surprised.

Loch realizes how ridiculous his question sounds but he doesn't have the strength to explain, and he now has a bigger concern to worry about. He cannot move his legs.

He tries to turn his body onto his side but his legs won't respond. In fact, he has no sensation whatsoever from the waist down, and he begins to think he's become paralyzed. *Could I have injured myself in the cargo net?* He remembers the net swinging, but it never crashed into the hull.

Slowly, he tries to move his legs again. First he tries to lift his left leg. Nothing. Then the right. Same result.

He's concerned but not panicked. He knows he's lucky to be alive and he simply can't process any more problems.

The lights in the room are bright, and Loch closes his salt-stained eyes to give them a rest. A minute later he feels the most glorious sensation. The ship's second officer is dabbing his cracked and parched lips with a damp cotton ball. Loch licks a single drop of water from his lips. Nothing has ever tasted so good.

"I need more water," Loch croaks.

"No, not yet. We will check with the captain."

Loch sighs. He keeps his eyes shut. He's gone without fluids for thirty hours, and he figures he can last another few minutes until the captain gives the OK.

A couple of minutes later he tastes something equally as good. The same officer is now dabbing his lips with tea. Loch savors the few drops of liquid he licks, thinking he has never had tea even remotely as good as this.

"What kind of tea is this?" Loch whispers. His eyes are still closed but he hears a couple of men exchange words.

A minute later a crewmember says, "This is the tea."

Loch opens his eyes and sees that the man is holding a box of Lipton.

Smiling, Loch starts to close his eyes again, but sees something on a small table about four feet away. Loch reaches toward it, but the object is too far. He is trying to grab a bottle of water. His thirst is unbearable.

Again the second officer says, "No. No water yet. Too soon. We are waiting for the captain to tell us when it will be OK."

Loch's head slumps, but he does not say anything. He knows that these men care about him and are still worried about his survival. He can see it in their eyes, hear it in their voices. And so he closes his eyes. He cannot, however, stop thinking about the bottle of water that is only four feet away. It reminds him of how close he was to the ship without being able to get on board.

Finally, word comes down from the captain that it is all right to give Loch a small quantity of water.

Loch watches as the second officer takes the bottle of water, fills a Dixie cup, and brings it to him. The water is so good, so pure, so sweet, it's indescribable. The life-giving fluid is such a relief from all the mouthfuls of dehydrating seawater he swallowed that he actually feels his body become both energized and relaxed. Loch wants more, but the second officer tells him to wait just a bit longer.

This time Loch drops his head on the pillow not out of exasperation, but from gratitude and a sense of well-being. He closes his eyes and is asleep within seconds.

For the families, the waiting since the original notification has been excruciating. The Coast Guard had been giving them periodic updates, but the first good news about any of the survivors was finally communicated on Sunday evening after Ron, Chris, and Kathy were safely in the helicopter. At about 8:30 p.m. Laura Ferrer, who was at a friend's house, received a call from her brother, who had been in touch with the Coast Guard.

Laura's brother said, "They have Chris! He's OK. He is on a Coast Guard helicopter."

Laura could barely believe the good news, making her brother repeat what little he knew over and over. The Coast Guard had said the helicopter was heading to Nantucket, so Laura started planning to drive to Hyannis and take a ferry over to the island. The ferries, however, weren't running because of high seas, so Laura instead started driving home.

At midnight, while Laura was still driving, her cell phone rang. It was Chris.

"Oh my God," said Laura. "Are you all right?"

Chris answered with his usual understated humor. "Couldn't be better. Eating a turkey sandwich right now. I'm at the Nantucket Hospital, and they are treating us like kings. I'll be able to catch a ferry over to Hyannis tomorrow and you can meet me there."

It would be another eight-hour wait for Laura, but this was a piece of cake: Chris really had survived.

Susan Burd, still in her hotel room alone in Atlanta, received her phone call about the same time as Laura. She was in tears, but elated and grateful. She tried to book a flight out of Atlanta that night but could not find one with an empty seat, so she took the first flight heading to Boston on Monday morning.

Just minutes after she arrived at her home in New Hampshire, Ron was at the front door. For Sue, seeing Ron walk through the door as if nothing had happened was a surreal sight—especially after thinking the worst just a few hours ago. After a tearful reunion, she had Ron tell her about the ordeal. At that point neither had the latest update on Tom or Loch, but both thought the chances of the two men still being alive were nearly impossible.

The story of the *Almeisan* was covered by newspapers, TV, radio, and the Internet that Monday. Some of the information was still incorrect due to the garbled radio communication between the *Almeisan* and the C-130 that found its way into the very first Coast Guard press release. One major newspaper started its story as follows:

> The U.S. Coast Guard was searching parts of the Atlantic Sunday for two men, one of them from Connecticut, who had abandoned a 45-foot sailboat in a storm about 400 miles off the Virginia coast. Lochlin Reidy, 58, of Woodbridge, and Thomas Tighe of Patterson, NY, abandoned the Almeisan for a covered life raft. . . . Three people who decided to stay with the *Almeisan* were rescued.
>
> A call made to Reidy's home in Woodbridge Sunday was not answered.

In her Connecticut home, Sandy Reidy did not return any calls from the media. She spent a sleepless night, knowing that as time passed there would be less and less of a chance of Loch's being found alive, or even being found at all. That's what logic told her. Yet her intuition was telling her he wasn't gone.

Then, at 6:30 a.m. a Coast Guard representative called. "Your husband has been found," said the spokesperson, "and he's alive."

"Is he OK?" asked Sandy.

"We don't know yet."

"Is Tom alive?"

"No."

The spokesperson asked Sandy to come to a Coast Guard station in nearby New Haven, for an update. They also said Anne Tighe would be there, but she had not yet been told about either Tom or Loch.

Sandy could not celebrate. Not only was Tom dead, she had no idea about Loch's situation. *What does alive mean?* she asked herself.

Anne Tighe had a night just as difficult as Sandy. She was relieved to learn that Ron, Kathy, and Chris were safe, but devastated after learning about the empty life raft. She tried to rest but kept thinking of Loch and Tom being battered by the seas. As the hours passed she became certain both men were dead; too much time had gone by.

In the morning she drove to the New Haven Coast Guard station with her two sons, and it was there that her worst fears were confirmed. Tom was dead.

Her family and friends helped her through this heartbreaking period, but there was something else that also gave her strength. She thought of Tom, and knew that what mattered most to him was the safety of his crew. And all four crewmembers were indeed alive. For that she was grateful.

CHAPTER THIRTY-THREE

"THIS IS REAL, THIS IS REAL"

Recovering Tom's body is a difficult task for the crewmembers of the *Sakura Express*. Even with the faint light of dawn, the crew loses sight of him in the foaming seas, and it takes several minutes to locate him again. Once he is spotted, the giant tanker slowly maneuvers toward Tom, trying not to run over him. As the tanker approaches two crewmembers get inside the cargo net, which has been formed into a makeshift basket, and they are lowered toward Tom. They try to grab hold of him. A giant wave surges beneath the net, and in an instant Tom has been pushed several feet away. Another wave breaks on Tom, and he is gone from sight.

Several minutes go by, with both the crew on deck and the two men in the cargo net scanning the waves for Tom. They know the victim has a life jacket on, and know that by now he must be back on the surface. But where?

Then a crewmember from the deck spots Tom, well aft of the men in the cargo net. Captain Tolja must once again try to reposition the vessel so his crew in the net has a shot at reaching Tom. Like Loch, Tolja has committed himself to bringing Tom home. He has vowed to himself that he will not leave the scene until they recover his fellow captain. But every time he has the boat positioned next to the body, a wave carries it away from the men in the net.

This exasperating scenario plays itself out over several times in the next hour. One of the crewmembers inside the cargo net is the chief engineer, a Slovenian named Herman Antonic, who decides he has seen enough and surprises everyone by risking his life and leaping into the maelstrom. Swimming to Tom, he grabs hold of the harness around the dead man and pulls him back toward the net. With the aid of the other crewmember they secure Tom to the net, and Antonic lunges back inside. The crane lifts them all up and safely deposits them on the deck. Tom is put in a body bag, covered with ice, and then secured on deck.

Down below in the small medical room, Loch has been sleeping for a few minutes, when suddenly he wakes with a start. The five crewmembers still in the room are startled, and they jump from their chairs and onto their feet.

Loch has no idea where he is. The lights have been turned down. He spots a porthole, then he sees the concerned faces of the Filipino crew, and for a split second fears he is hallucinating and is really still in the ocean.

The crewmembers see the terror in Loch's face and one of them holds the survivor's hand, reassuring him. Loch calms down and readjusts. *This is real, this is real. I'm OK.*

Crewmembers give Loch more water, which he greedily gulps down. Minutes later Captain Tolja comes down and asks Loch how he is feeling. Loch says he's doing good, all things considered. The captain tells Loch they have recovered Tom's body. Loch lets out a long sigh. It would have been heartrending to have gone through all the hours of struggle to keep Tom with him, only to have him lost at sea at the very time Loch was rescued.

There are tears in Loch's eyes. He has fulfilled the promise he made to Tom during the worst of the storm. He would bring Tom home.

Loch tries to move his right leg, and as before there is no response. But when he tries his left leg he gets it to move a bit. He now knows he's not paralyzed, and he lets himself sink down into the bed and doze.

When he wakes, about forty-five minutes have gone by, and the captain, who has been alerted that Loch is no longer sleeping, reenters the room.

Of Croatian descent, Captain Srdan Tolja is forty-seven years old. He is a tall, trim man, with short brown-gray hair, and he dresses in casual clothes like the rest of the crew. "It is still very rough out," says the captain in English with a heavy accent. "We are going to have

185

to move your captain from one side of the ship to the other because the waves are breaking over the side he is on. Is that OK with you?"

Already Loch likes this man, who goes out of his way to show respect. "Of course," Loch says, "whatever you have to do is fine."

A crewmember tells Loch they have all their deck lights on. Loch does not understand. It is 7 a.m. and although there is still a low cloud cover, it is nothing like the darkness of night.

Loch asks why the lights are on. The crewmember explains this is a Filipino custom when someone dies. At home they turn their lights on when someone has passed away.

Loch nods, envisioning the deck above, glowing. And as if to remind him that a storm is still raging, the ship takes a wave hard and Loch feels the vessel shudder and hears the thump from the sea slamming the hull.

Again Loch falls back to sleep, and when he wakes it is 8:30 a.m.

"Would you like to eat breakfast?" asks a crewmember.

Thinking he can order breakfast Loch says, "Yes, please. I'd like eggs, home fries, toast, and bacon."

The crewmembers look at each other, and two sailors leave the room to get Loch his breakfast. When they return they are carrying a bowl. Loch props himself on his side in the bed, and the crewmembers place the bowl in his left hand. In the bowl is mushroom soup.

Loch dips the spoon in, puts it in his mouth, and smiles. The hot soup is the absolute best.

As soon as he is finished, another crewmember returns with a large platter. It is heaped with mashed potatoes, enough for everybody in the room. Loch hesitates but the crew encourages him to start eating. Loch isn't really hungry after the soup but he doesn't want to say anything that might remotely offend anyone. He is growing close to these sailors who obviously have his best interests in mind. They seem like the most caring people on earth. And so Loch starts eating the mashed potatoes, and stays with it until two-thirds of the potatoes have been consumed.

"Let's celebrate," says a crewmember. "How about a beer?"

For Loch to say no to a beer would be like the sun not coming up. Yet, for the first time in his life, he pauses. Then he says yes, again not wanting to appear ungrateful.

The crewmember leaves to get the drinks, and Loch expects him to return with Filipino-brand beers. Instead he comes back with two Heinekens. The crewmember opens one for Loch and one for himself. He raises his beer toward Loch, and Loch, now propped up in the bed, returns the toast.

Loch wonders about drinking the beer on top of all the mushroom soup and potatoes he's eaten, but he pushes the concern aside while he looks at the smiling faces watching him. He takes a long swig. The beer is warm, but that's fine with Loch. Over the next two minutes Loch drinks most of the beer, then puts it down and promptly falls back to sleep.

When Loch wakes up near noontime, the captain is summoned. Captain Tolja asks how Loch is feeling.

"I'm doing good," says Loch. Then he asks, "Where are we going?"

"We're heading to Boston, then on to New York City."

"Boston and New York sound good."

The captain gives Loch an odd look, knowing that Loch will be dropped off at their first port. He doesn't spell this out for Loch but instead says, "We will be arriving in Boston tomorrow at about 8 a.m."

Loch understands he will depart in Boston.

A crewmember enters the room and in his arms he has Loch's jeans, T-shirt, and white socks, all freshly washed. Loch tries to get out of bed but is unable to stand. His right knee is especially causing pain, and he knows sometime during the battering by the seas he has wrenched his knee. He lies back on the bed, and the crewmember covers Loch with blankets and then says, "Lunchtime."

Loch, not learning from his breakfast order, quickly exclaims, "Boy, I'd love to have a hamburger." He's been thinking about a hamburger quite frequently, because when he was on the *Almeisan* he and Kathy talked about the first thing they would eat when they arrived in Bermuda, which was a simple hamburger. And as the storm deepened they started expanding on the hamburger, first making it a cheeseburger, then adding onions. By the height of the storm they had loaded it with pickles, lettuce, tomato, and bacon, as well as French fries on the side and much more.

But Loch quickly realizes he's not in a restaurant, and says, "Never mind the hamburger, I should have asked what's for lunch."

"Fish," says the crewmember.

Of all the possible lunch options this is the least attractive for Loch. He does not want to eat anything connected with the water. But instead, he nods politely, and says, "That will be good."

The crewmember heads to the galley and returns with a large plate. On it is a beautiful piece of salmon, along with vegetables and a boiled potato. He also has a milk glass filled with red wine. Loch is not at all sure he can drink the wine or even get down a mouthful of potato, but he surprises himself by consuming the entire lunch and drinking all the wine. Then he feels too tired to keep his eyes open and it's back to sleep. He sleeps on and off throughout the afternoon, and groggily notices how any time one of his arms emerges from the blankets, one of the three remaining crewmembers hovering over him immediately covers it back up.

When he finally wakes for good, it is 5 p.m. and one of the crewmembers cheerfully says, "It's dinnertime!"

This time Loch knows better than to order. He doesn't think he can eat another bite of food, and wonders how safe it is to be eating so much, especially having gone without food for more than sixty hours before his rescue. But when he sees the happiness on the face of the crewmember who returns with a plate of steak tips, vegetables, and yet more potatoes, Loch thinks to himself, *What the heck.* And again, he finds the dinner is good, and does it justice. He does the same to the glass of wine that accompanies the dinner.

After dinner the medic takes his temperature and blood pressure, and says all is well. The captain visits briefly and in the course of their conversation, he tells Loch the weather is still bad and they won't reach Boston until 10 a.m. the following day.

That gets Loch to thinking about Boston. He incorrectly guesses that no one besides the Coast Guard even knows about his accident, and thinks he will simply be dropped off on a pier in Boston. *How will I get home? I don't even have any shoes.*

Loch only knows two people in Boston, Erica Robertson and Colby Brunt, both good friends he knows he can count on. He starts to formulate a plan. When he departs from the *Sakura Express,* he will call these two friends. And when contact is made with one of them, he will ask to borrow money so he can catch a train from Boston to

New Haven and then call his wife. *But will the government even let me off the ship? I have no passport. And what will I do with Tom?*

A crewmember takes Loch's mind off the dilemma by bringing him the loose change that was found in the survivor's pocket. "May I keep the quarter with the sailboat on it?" the crewmember asks. "I want to make a necklace to remember you by."

"Of course," answers Loch, thinking he would give these men every penny he had if they ever needed it.

The wine, the food, and his lack of strength from his hours in the ocean catch up with him. He closes his eyes and does not wake until morning.

As soon as he stirs a crewmember says, "Breakfast time!"

Almost immediately, a tray of food is brought to him. This time he gets his eggs, toast, and sausage, along with the usual heaping mound of mashed potatoes. He is also given a glass of orange juice. Loch figures he'll take a couple of bites, but again he is shocked at how hungry he is and how good the food tastes, and he eats it all.

I better stop eating like this, thinks Loch, *I'm going to return home with more weight on me than when I left.*

He also mulls over his return to Boston once again. He anticipates having to ask his rescuers to arrange to have a wheelchair waiting for him, because he believes he will never walk again.

189

CHAPTER THIRTY-FOUR

THE POWER OF LITTLE STEPS

After breakfast, Captain Tolja arrives in the medical room and he and Loch have a long talk. First the captain says that the weather is still bad out, and now the estimated time of arrival in Boston has been pushed back to noon. Then he tells Loch more about the rescue, pointing out that four C-130s were involved, and how the Navy ship *Seay* stayed on scene helping coordinate the vessels that were part of the AMVER program. The captain says that in addition to the *Sakura Express,* the other AMVER vessels were the *Castillo de Butrón* and the *Front Brabant,* which were searching different areas of the ocean. He also relates how excited he was when the *Sakura* approached the life raft and how disappointed he was after finding it empty.

Loch digests the information as best he can. While in the water it was his faith in the Coast Guard rescue efforts that helped keep him going, but he had no idea how many planes and ships were involved. He thinks about his excruciatingly slow paddle around the entire *Sakura,* and asks, "What about the mechanical noise I heard in the water near the *Sakura*? Was that the bow thrusters?"

"No," answers Tolja. "That must have been the motor on the crane. We were getting it and the net ready for you."

Loch nods, pausing to consider all the frantic kicking to escape what he thought were the whirling propellers of the bow thrusters. He does not berate himself, because he knows at the time that he didn't have the luxury to stop and try to figure out the source of the noise.

The two men talk a little more about the ship, and Captain Tolja asks Loch if there is anything he can do for him at the moment.

Loch surprises the captain by saying, "I think I'd like to try and stand up now."

The captain and another man stand by the side of the survivor's bed.

Gingerly, Loch pivots and carefully moves both legs to the edge of the bed. He is able to sit up with the lower part of his legs dangling off the bed. It is the first time he has sat since he was thrown out of the life raft, and it gives him confidence to try to rise.

With the captain and a crewmember providing a bit of support under each arm, Loch slowly stands. Then he takes a stiff, tentative step with his left leg. Then with his right. There is pain in his knee, but the leg does not buckle. With the aid of his helpers he takes four more steps to a table, rests, then takes five more steps back to his bed. He plops down into a sitting position, exhausted but triumphant, raising both fists in the air. Laughs and cheers erupt from the crewmembers in the room. Loch answers with an ear-to-ear smile. It is a special moment, one that he will never forget.

More crewmembers arrive in the room. A couple of sailors have cameras and want their picture taken with the miracle man, their new friend. Everyone is joking and smiling as the camera flashes shine on the men.

While the picture-taking session is going on, Captain Tolja slips from the room and returns with a toothbrush, toothpaste, shampoo, razor, and shaving cream. He points toward the bathroom connected to the room and says, "Whenever you're ready there is a shower and towel in there. We have plenty of hot water."

Loch lets the words "hot water" sink in a bit, then he says, "I'm ready!"

Two crewmembers help him to the bathroom, and tell him just to call if he needs anything. When they shut the door, Loch looks in the mirror. He barely recognizes the disheveled, ancient-looking face staring back at him. He's got a five-day growth of stubbly beard, his lips are cracked, and his skin red and chafed. The green eyes gazing back are sunk deep in their sockets, and despite all his sleep there are bags under Loch's eyes.

Well what did you expect? Loch asks himself. He brushes his teeth, then slowly shaves, missing at least half his whiskers. *Enough of this, let's get in that shower.*

Once the water coming from the showerhead is good and hot, Loch inches his way in. He lets the water wash over him and does not move. This sensation is right up there with the tea being dabbed on his lips. The salt, which seems to have been pounded into every pore, slowly rinses away. He stands in the shower a full five minutes, letting its warmth seep into his bones. He can feel himself getting drowsy, and quickly washes up.

After he dries himself off and wraps a towel around his waist, he hobbles from the bathroom, feeling spent from the fifteen minutes of standing. The three crewmembers waiting for him smile and nod, an acknowledgment that he's well on his way to recovery. They help him to bed, pull the covers over him, and Loch falls asleep.

He sleeps for two hours until late morning and when he awakes, Captain Tolja returns.

"Our progress north is slow," says Captain Tolja. "We have passed Long Island, but won't reach Boston until afternoon."

"I'm in no rush," says Loch. All the delays are actually good for Loch, because they give him more time to readjust before the crush of civilization. Having gone through a traumatic situation—much of it tethered to Tom in the open sea—his time on the *Sakura* is allowing him to decompress. He needs to adjust before reentering his former reality and the buzz of a city.

"Would you like to see the rest of the ship and the bridge?" asks the captain.

"Yes," says Loch, "that would be great."

Loch sits at the edge of the bed, and, at a snail's pace, puts on his clean T-shirt, jeans, and socks. Captain Tolja passes him a pair of black sneakers, probably the captain's own.

Once Loch has the sneakers on, the captain helps him stand and together they carefully shuffle toward the engine room. "Do you think you can make it down these steps?" asks Captain Tolja.

"Let's give it a shot," answers Loch. By putting most of his weight on his good leg, getting down the flight of stairs is not as difficult as Loch thought it would be, although he does wonder how he will get back up.

Any concerns vanish when he sees the massive engine room. The sight of cylinders as big as automobiles is something he has never seen before, and he is even more surprised to count only four of the enormous cylinders. Every piece of steel shines in the spotless room.

The ship's second officer, a Filipino named Erwin Salvoza, is in the engine room, and gladly answers all of Loch's questions. Loch is fascinated by the inner workings of the *Sakura* as the men discuss the mechanics of the ship.

Then it's on to the bridge. Going up the steps leading out of the engine room is indeed more difficult and Loch takes frequent rests, his right knee causing him considerable pain. As he hobbles toward the bridge he notes that the entire ship is immaculate, and learns from the captain that the *Sakura Express* was built just two years earlier.

When they enter the bridge, Loch again forgets his physical limitations and discomfort, because he now understands how he could have been so close to the vessel without the crew spotting him. The ship is so gigantic that there are plenty of blind spots extending dozens of feet beyond the hull. Couple that with the crashing seas and Loch realizes just how lucky he was that his shouts were heard and that he was then spotted by a crewmember.

The captain shows Loch a weather fax of the storm, received just a few minutes earlier. Although the ship is now sailing through better weather, the storm, which has moved northeast, is still massive, stretching from Nova Scotia south toward Georges Bank. There have been more powerful storms to come up the eastern seaboard, but few have covered such an enormous portion of the ocean.

Looking out one of the windows on the port side, Loch notices a lighthouse tower far in the distance.

"Is that the Race Point Light at Provincetown?" asks Loch.

"Yes," says Captain Tolja. "Not too long before we reach Boston."

While Loch cannot spot land, seeing the top half of the lighthouse is his first glimpse in a week of any land-based structure. He simply stares toward the lighthouse, his emotions confused, feeling as if he's not ready for whatever will happen once he steps off the ship. *We really are going to Boston, and we'll be there soon . . .*

After his tour of the bridge, Loch rests in the officers' cabin. Soon Captain Tolja returns and says, "Let's have some lunch."

Loch feels like he's eaten triple what he might consume on a cruise trip, but he follows the captain down to the mess hall. Once inside, he and the captain join a couple of other officers in their section of the mess hall, and are served salmon with vegetables. Again Loch is surprised that he still has an appetite. After dinner he limps into the small galley, thanking the chefs for all they have done.

Next, he and Captain Tolja take a couple of steps across the galley, and emerge in the crew side of the mess hall, where they sit down with some of the sailors.

"Do you know you are famous?" asks one of the crewmembers.

"No, I'm not famous," says Loch.

"Yes you are; come with me."

The crewmember leads Loch and the captain into a small lounge for the crew, where there is a TV. "Just a few minutes ago we saw your picture on TV, followed by a story of what happened on the *Almeisan*. And there are news reporters waiting for you in Boston."

Loch is taken aback. All along he was thinking no one outside the Coast Guard knew what happened. He is now quite anxious about this turn of events, and Captain Tolja sees it in the survivor's face.

"Don't worry, once we are in Boston Harbor the Coast Guard will come out on one of their boats and bring you in. We are too loaded to go in directly and must anchor in the harbor."

Loch spends the next few minutes sitting in the lounge, trying to get a grip on this news. He begins to realize that his family must know what happened, and maybe he won't have to call his two Boston friends and ask for money. He lies down on the couch in the lounge and briefly dozes.

A short time later, the *Sakura Express* steams into Boston Harbor, drops anchor and Captain Tolja communicates, via VHF radio, with three Coast Guard patrol boats that arrive at the ship.

The gangway is lowered and three Coast Guardsmen board the ship and walk down to the lounge, where they greet Loch warmly.

One of the men is a medical officer, who performs a quick exam of the survivor, takes his blood pressure, and asks a few questions related to how he is feeling. He asks Loch about his aching knee and makes sure Loch is not experiencing pain anywhere else in his body. Then a Lieutenant Muñoz, a young man in his early thirties, sits down with Loch in the lounge and explains to him that he needs to get a brief statement about what happened. Lieutenant Muñoz asks Loch to begin at the point when they first left Bridgeport, and as Loch takes him through the events leading up to his being thrown from the life raft, the lieutenant jots down notes. He listens carefully, nodding in a sympathetic way, letting Loch describe how Tom died, how one of the C-130s eventually located him, and his trouble being seen by the crewmembers on the *Sakura*. After fifteen minutes, Muñoz decides he has enough information, concerned that the retelling of the event could be exhausting Loch.

As soon as Muñoz closes his notebook, he explains to Loch that they will go topside to a waiting patrol boat and begin the process of getting him to a hospital. Muñoz and the medic help Loch stand and ask him if needs assistance walking. Loch says he is OK, but the two Coast Guardsmen stay close to Loch, especially when Loch inches his way up the stairs. Once on deck, Loch can see there are two forty-one-foot Coast Guard boats circling slowly below, and one forty-seven-foot Coast Guard boat holding position closer to the ship.

Lieutenant Muñoz says, "We will take you to the Coast Guard station in Boston and then an ambulance will bring you to Mass General Hospital. Do you think you can get off the ship to one of our boats?"

Loch can only see a rope ladder, and while staring at it, says, "No way."

Muñoz smiles. "No, no, no, not the ladder. The ship has a gangway with a railing."

Loch now remembers the gangway, the same one he tried to ride a wave up to and considered grabbing hold of, before he realized he'd be crushed.

Almost the entire crew of the *Sakura Express* has gathered around Loch, and each man shakes his hand, gives him a hug, and wishes him the best. Loch starts to choke up, and can barely respond. He feels such goodwill toward the crew that he has mixed emotions about leaving the vessel.

He limps toward the gangway and looks down at the Coast Guard boat below. On it is a Coast Guard photographer. Before Loch takes his first step, he starts to steel himself for reentry into the fray of civilization.

CHAPTER THIRTY-FIVE

GOOD-BYES

Now as Loch takes his first tentative step onto the gangplank, he fights back an upwelling of tears. With his hands tight on the railings, and a Coastie in front of and behind him, he limps down to the waiting patrol boat. At the end of the gangway is a platform and next to that the patrol boat bobs in the three-foot chop. Loch hesitates before boarding the boat, thinking that with his bad leg he could very well end up in the water.

Lieutenant Muñoz senses Loch's uncertainty. "We'll assist you onto the boat. Why don't you put on a life jacket?"

"That's a good idea," answers Loch, slipping on a PFD. As Loch haltingly puts one leg out toward the boat, helping hands from the patrol boat crew steady him as he boards.

An eruption of clapping and cheering comes from above. Startled, Loch looks up at the *Sakura*'s deck, where the entire crew is lining the rail, celebrating Loch's achievement of being safely in the hands of the Coast Guard. Loch waves at the men and they continue clapping. He then hugs the Coasties on the boat, saying how grateful he is for everything the Coast Guard did for him.

One of the Coast Guardsmen, apparently forgetting that Loch kept himself tethered to his dead captain for several hours, says, "Do you want to go in alone or with Tom?"

"With Tom," answers Loch.

The *Sakura*'s crane swings into action, and Tom's body is lowered onto the boat.

Loch takes a seat and the boat pulls away from the ship, motoring toward Boston. The other two patrol boats follow, and Loch takes a final look back at the *Sakura,* its orange hull shining in the sunlight.

The crewmembers who helped save his life and took such good care of him are now just specks up on the deck.

It's a short ride to the Coast Guard station in Boston, and when the flotilla arrives, Loch notices a helicopter circling overhead.

"That's a TV helicopter," says one the Coasties. "This is a big story."

Two EMTs are waiting at the dock as Loch is escorted off the boat.

"Let's get you on a stretcher," one of the technicians says.

"I'm OK, thanks, I can walk."

While the technician fastens a soft brace around Loch's right knee he says, "When we get you to Mass General you're going to be registered under an assumed name. There's a million reporters waiting by the entrance, but we won't let them get to you."

Loch can't quite get his mind around this. *Why is this a big story?*

Sure enough, when they arrive at the hospital they do pass a horde of reporters. When the ambulance comes to a stop by the emergency room entrance, Loch hears reporters shouting questions at him from the front of the building. They are kept back and Loch can barely hear what they are saying. Then he sees his daughters, Denise and Ashley, running to him. They all embrace, and the girls won't let him go. A few seconds later he is reunited with his wife, Sandy.

Into the hospital they all go and sit in a hallway with the other emergency room patients. A nurse checks Loch's blood pressure and temperature, and tells him he will soon be admitted. Several minutes go by. Loch doesn't feel like he needs a complete examination, and just wants to go home. Finally Denise has had enough of the waiting and goes to the admissions desk and explains that her father is the man they should have been expecting, the man who just spent the last twenty-five hours in the sea. The woman at the desk apologizes, explaining that because he was registered under an assumed name, there was a mix-up and they didn't know he was the survivor they had been told about.

The family is brought to a private room. Loch's friends Susan and Jack Cary arrive, saying that they were driving to Maine, heard the news report about Loch on the radio, and headed straight to Mass General. The Carys weren't sure what to expect, but considering the amount of time Loch was in the ocean, they say he looks great.

Next Loch is taken for an MRI on his knee and while he waits for the procedure, he overhears a nurse talking to a coworker.

"I'm absolutely drowning in work," she says. Then she gasps, realizing who Loch is. "I'm so sorry," she says to Loch, "that was a poor choice of words."

"No worries," says Loch. "I know how you feel!"

While waiting for the MRI, Loch falls asleep. When he opens his eyes a few minutes later someone is holding his hand. It's Colby Brunt, the very friend in Boston whom Loch was going to call if the *Sakura* dropped him off at a pier. She heard the news on TV and rushed over to the hospital. (Later, Loch learns that the other Boston friend he was going to contact, Erica Robertson, also heard about his plight from the news, and she arrived at the Coast Guard station just as Loch was being helped into the ambulance. Both friends were there for him, and he never even made a phone call.)

Once the MRI is finished, Loch is refitted with a leg brace and a doctor informs him that he has minor ligament damage, which may heal on its own, but he should follow up with a doctor near home. Then he is released. The drive home seems a bit dreamlike, as Loch watches people racing in their cars, all hurrying for their own reasons. On the Massachusetts Turnpike the family stops at the Charlton rest area, and again Loch stares at people scurrying around the fast food restaurants. The pace of civilization, and the seemingly meaningless rushing, makes Loch think that if these people thought about how fragile life is, they'd all slow down and enjoy it more. Even when Loch gets home and lies down in his own bed he cannot sleep right away; it's as if he was never part of this modern world, never part of this frenetic culture.

Yet what he has experienced so far on land is nothing compared to what's coming.

When Loch hobbles out of bed the next morning, Wednesday, May 11, his daughter Ashley brings him to the window in the front of the house. The street is jammed with cars, TV news vans, and reporters mingling about. As Loch stares incredulously, the phone starts ringing. It is the first of more than four dozen calls that pour in throughout the day.

But Loch has a call of his own to make. He dials the Tighes' home number and talks with Anne. He doesn't spare any details, telling her how Tom died, how he tried to give him his last rites, and how sorry he was he couldn't have done more. Loch also describes how Tom tried to give him his life jacket when he knew he probably wasn't going to make it. Loch and Anne make it a point to meet soon.

After the phone call, Ashley says, "What do you want to do with all those reporters out there?"

Loch surprises her by responding, "I don't mind them. In fact I'll talk with them. Why don't you find out who was here first, and I'll start with that reporter. You can bring them into the kitchen or we can talk out on the deck."

"Are you sure you want to do that?"

"Let's give it a try and see how it goes. I'd rather they get the story right than run articles based on hearsay and speculation."

And so, one by one, over the course of the entire day, Loch talks to each and every reporter. He does not find the experience draining, but instead finds the process interesting and the reporters professional. When discussing the *Sakura Express,* he makes sure the reporters know how compassionately he was treated, and he explains that if the ship had not been part of the AMVER program he'd still be in the ocean. He even lets his sense of humor come through by telling one reporter that the jeans he is wearing are the ones he had on during the ordeal, adding, "They are ocean-washed Levi's, they were tumbled quite often."

The next few days are a time to rest and readjust. On Sunday, May 15, Loch attends Tom's wake. Kathy, Ron, and Chris are all there, and Loch is delighted to see them. The wake is packed with family, friends, sailing buddies, and coworkers. Anne Tighe, Tom's wife, is doing as well as can be expected. She's been feeling numb and on automatic pilot, but she's been blessed with three grown children, Cathy, Tom, and Peter, who have not only provided Anne with strength and love but have assisted with the funeral arrangements. Each of the children, as well as Anne, have been on different Bermuda trips with Tom, and each can't help but think, *Could I have changed the outcome if I had gone on that trip?* Logically they know their presence would likely not have affected the result, but that feeling is quite common among family members of a loved one who has died at sea, or died in a setting with which the family was familiar.

The next day is the funeral at the Tighes' parish church, and afterward the attendees spend time remembering Tom at a local Irish pub. Doug and Jill Griffin, friends and shipmates of the Tighes, present a slide presentation of happier days, and several people speak of fond memories of the captain.

In accordance with Tom's wishes he is cremated and his ashes are returned to the family for burial at sea. Tom's daughter Cathy arranges the burial details, obtaining an urn and even preparing a heart-shaped silver locket for each family member with Tom's picture and a small amount of his ashes inside.

Because the *Almeisan* has been berthed for several years at Captain's Cove Marina on Black Rock Harbor in Bridgeport, Connecticut, the family decides that's the area where his ashes should be buried. They remember the mouth of Black Rock Harbor as Tom's gateway—coming and going—to Bermuda, or Long Island, or east to the Race, or west to Hell's Gate, or in between. Anne considers it the perfect spot because Tom loved every inch of that waterway.

On the day of the burial, Captain's Cove Marina provides a boat with a canopy for the sea ceremony. Family, friends, and, of course, Loch, are all on board. Several people briefly speak about their experiences with Tom, then they all pray, before casting the urn and flowers into the sea.

Loch has one last matter he feels he absolutely must take care of. He wants to thank the *Sakura Express* crewmembers. First he needs to find the ship. He recalls that it was heading to New York and New Jersey after Boston, and he telephones both Coast Guard and AMVER officials to locate the vessel. They help put Loch in touch with the ship's broker, who is able to pinpoint the time when the ship will be off-loading in Linden, New Jersey. Next, Loch has to scramble to find a gift, a token of his appreciation. He decides to give the officers wine made in their own countries, and after a little searching finds what he needs. And for the crew he wants to buy them Filipino beer. This proves tougher than the wine, because there has been a recent embargo on certain Filipino products, and beer is one of them. He asks his daughter Denise if she has any ideas, and she says, "Why don't I ask all my friends to check the various liquor stores near where they live. There must still be some around if we look hard enough." After searching dozens of stores, Denise and friends find ten cases.

Once the beer is at Denise's home in Hoboken, New Jersey, Loch and his family drive down to her home early the next morning. They pick up Denise and her husband, Mark, and then make one more stop before driving to the terminal. Driving to Battery Park in New York, they stop at the AMVER office, where two of the coordinators are thrilled to caravan down to the *Sakura*. One of the men is Benjamin Strong, who heads up AMVER coordination with the Coast Guard and whom Loch has gotten to know over the phone.

When the group arrives at the Citgo Marine Terminal in Linden, the manager is waiting for them. He explains that because of security Loch will not be able to go on board the *Sakura,* but that the captain and a handful of crew (who have the necessary paperwork to disembark) are waiting at the main office. They all drive to the office, and carry the beer and wine inside. It's a wonderful reunion. Loch presents Captain Tolja with the gifts, and then from a paper bag he pulls out the black sneakers that were given to him on board the ship. The captain smiles in astonishment, shaking his head.

For the next hour everyone enjoys the reunion, but Loch feels something is missing. He walks over to the terminal manager and says, "How can I see the rest of the crew?"

The manager, who has gone out of his way to be helpful, answers, "Well, we can't let you on the vessel, but follow me."

Loch and his family hop in the manager's car and are driven to a pier, where Loch sees the familiar orange hull of the *Sakura Express.* It triggers a fleeting vision of the ship while he swam a complete circle around it, wondering if he would ever be saved.

The manager toots his horn several times. The beer and wine are carried up the gangway. Loch steps out of the car, looks up at the deck, and sees crewmembers running to the rail. They start waving and cheering at Loch and his family.

A feeling of love and gratitude sweeps over Loch. This time he does not try to control the tears, but instead smiles through the emotion and waves good-bye.

AUTHOR'S NOTE AND ACKNOWLEDGMENTS

A reader once asked me, "Do you only write disaster books?" It was a good question, because my last three offerings—*Fatal Forecast, Ten Hours Until Dawn,* and *The Finest Hours*—could qualify as weather-related disaster books. But it's not the storms or even the ensuing calamity that really interests me so much as the people. All three of those books document ordinary people thrust into incredibly difficult situations where they have to rise to the challenge, persevere, and fight against long odds. Consequently, I'm careful about what book projects I take on, because the core of the story must be about people, and since I'll be working with these people quite closely, we have to click and build trust. In the case of *Overboard,* I was blessed to partner with sailors and Coasties who more than met those criteria and, as an added bonus, became my friends.

The genesis of *Overboard* was different than for my other books: instead of me finding the story, it found me. Ron Burd came to a slide presentation I was giving on *Fatal Forecast* at a library. At the end of the program, when the librarian and I were packing up, Ron introduced himself and explained that just a month earlier he had been involved in a life-and-death situation at sea. He gave me a brief overview of what happened, and I was hooked. A few weeks later I drove up to Ron's house in New Hampshire and we discussed his ill-fated voyage to Bermuda in detail. Ron was so helpful and precise in his explanations that I knew this project was meant to be and that the story would appeal to people outside the boating community. So to Ron, a big thank-you, for first calling my attention to this story and getting me started.

Chris Ferrer lives just forty-five minutes from my home, and we met shortly after my visit with Ron. My interview with Chris didn't take too long, since he had written a thorough witness statement for the Coast Guard investigators, which proved very helpful to me. Chris never said this, but I will; it's a damn good thing he was on the boat. When Kathy was swept overboard in the first knockdown, Ron was injured by the chart table, and Tom and Loch had all they could do to hang onto Kathy. Chris provided that third set of hands to haul her on board. Later, during the second knockdown, Ron was hurled from the boat, hanging onto a lifeline, and again it was Chris's strong hands that helped get him back on deck. In the beginning days of the voyage Chris may not have pulled his weight due to seasickness, but he recovered in time to come through in the clutch. He also provided moments of welcome humor, both for his fellow crew during the most tense moments of the catastrophe, and then again later for me as we worked together.

Kathy showed a steadiness and calmness in a situation that likely would have had me close to panic. I guess you just don't know how you will react until you are in a truly dire circumstance, but Kathy can rest assured that her crewmates vouched for her nerve. She took the voyage to learn everything she could about blue-water sailing, and she came away with more knowledge than some sailors acquire in a lifetime. And she taught me to always listen to your gut feelings. Before the *Almeisan* even left the dock, Kathy was having misgivings, thinking that it was too early in the season to make such a long voyage. She had even considered canceling prior to the trip, but due to her strong sense of commitment went ahead anyway. Her sense of unease increased dramatically when she heard the warning from the captain of another sailboat near Montauk, and she thought it would be easy enough for Tom to drop her off at one of the Long Island ports. But again she felt a sense of loyalty and responsibility to be the fifth crewmember. That same sense of conscientiousness showed itself during the writing of this book, when she patiently answered all my questions, even though it must have been difficult to relive such a traumatic experience.

I remember thinking how well these three individuals got along and worked as a team. They all added a personal strength, a key bit of advice, or a discovery that helped keep them alive. And, amazingly, there was not a single argument—not an easy feat when you haven't slept in days and every decision is critical. In the summer of 2008, I had a chance to see how well Chris and Ron crewed together when the three of us made an afternoon sail through Boston Harbor on Chris's boat. I remember hearing them both say they would consider a return sailing voyage to Bermuda, and I was astounded. Right after the accident both men said they doubted they would undertake another Bermuda-bound passage, so I asked them what had changed. They said they had learned so much on that trip and had had time to reflect that in some sense the voyage was unfinished business, and if the right opportunity came along they would consider it. Now, I've got to tip my hat to that notion, because had I survived the *Almeisan,* I would have moved to Omaha to be a good distance from the ocean!

Loch and I spent a lot of time together, and at the end of each session my respect for the man grew yet again. Besides recounting his ordeal, he had the added burden of speaking for Tom. We felt it was imperative that anything written about Tom could be verified by Loch. The two men were close friends, and because Loch had sailed with Tom to Bermuda more than anyone else, Loch could provide insight into the captain's planning, thinking, and risk analysis. It was important for me to make sure the reader understood that it wasn't just Tom who thought the *Almeisan* was sinking, but Loch also. Tom even asked Loch if he agreed with his assessment to deploy the life raft. There are sailors who will question Tom and Loch's decision, but they weren't on the battered boat in the middle of the storm when a judgment had to be made quickly.

Another person who made numerous voyages to Bermuda with Tom is Ray Knell, former commodore of the Annapolis Naval Sailing Association, who wrote, "Tom lived to teach and practice preparation, safety, and love of the ocean. He was the best person I knew at preparing for all eventualities at sea." That same sentiment was echoed by many people who had sailed with Tom. Ray Knell also pointed out that when EPIRB was activated on the *Almeisan* it alerted the Coast Guard of the emergency, but the device failed to give a position. Fortunately, logistician Donna Christman had received frequent calls from Tom updating her on the boat's longitude and latitude. "Because Tom called back to a shoreside contact at least daily with a position report," said Ray, "the other four persons on board survived."

Extra insight into understanding Tom and the workings of the *Almeisan* were provided by his gracious wife, Anne, and daughter, Cathy Chamberlain. To their credit they never asked to see what I was writing, but instead trusted that Loch and I would simply tell the story the way it happened. Cathy Chamberlain's only wish was that sailors who read the book learn from some of the revelations Loch and Tom discovered the hard way, such as having swimming goggles in their ditch bags and the need for life rafts to have more "hand-friendly" tethers. Although personal EPIRBs were not that common in 2005, they are readily available today at reasonable prices and should be considered by all blue-water mariners. And Anne Tighe helped me greatly with the final chapter, while also providing me with photos of Tom, Loch, and the *Almeisan*.

During my initial meetings with Loch at my home I tape-recorded my interviews with him. But in the later stages—covering the section of the story when Loch was in the ocean—we tried something I wasn't sure was going to work. Loch suggested that he write what happened to him and Tom in the first couple of hours after they were swept off the boat. When I later read what he wrote, I saw the wisdom of the idea. Loch is a good writer, and I believe that by allowing him to write rather than constantly speak about the event, he was able to add more detail, more thoughts, and more raw emotion. I was able to put Loch's recollections into my own voice to maintain consistency of narrative style throughout the book.

My goal was to establish a sense of immediacy and have the reader, particularly in the last third of the book, experience the ordeal as if he were there, looking out at the mountainous seas from Loch's green eyes. Where we succeeded, the credit goes to Loch, because he had to mine some painful emotions and lay bare his soul. To be sure, there were times during his tribulation when he was gripped by sheer terror or sank into despair. Courage does not mean the absence of these feelings, but rather mustering the will to keep going just a little longer, doing the best you can despite the fear. At no point was he immobilized by the hopelessness of the situation, and that is a big part of why he is alive.

Looking back on the flow of events, the reader first learns about Loch's gumption and determination when he unhooked the safety line to his harness and dove into the raft to try to get it closer to the boat. And months later, during the writing of this book, he used that same determination to explore every angle of his highs and lows, from the moment he was sent flying from the raft, through the darkest night of his life, to the many near-misses of planes and ships, and ultimate salvation.

During one of our get-togethers, I asked Loch how the survival ordeal had changed him or his outlook. He thought about that question for a long time, then said there had been no drastic changes in the way he lives or thinks. He did, however, point out a subtle shift in his perspective on life and reaction to events. "I now never fret over the little things. There's just too much good out there to waste time on issues that really are not all that important."

Bob Cummings, captain of the *At Ease,* has an outlook similar to Loch's. He's kept a pragmatic view of his experience, knowing that he and Jerry McCarthy did the right thing by abandoning the boat. "Anything could have happened had we stayed on the vessel; not just drowning but also injury—broken ribs, punctured lung, losing a finger. None of that was worth risking for a boat. We only have one body, but I could always get another boat." He also credits Jerry for helping with their survival. "When I was drained, Jerry was there. He just stepped up, and it's good to know there are people you can depend on."

In a separate conversation with Jerry, he recalled how well he and Bob meshed when the storm was throwing all it had at the *At Ease.* He later wrote to me and said, "I consider Bob like a brother. You go through something like that and you work so well together, you can't help but become close."

Bob's lasting memory of the ordeal was looking down from the helicopter immediately after he was hoisted on board. He wrote to me and explained it this way:

As we flew away I saw *At Ease* for the last time. She was sailing away in 30-foot seas headed for a destination I would never know. I like to imagine she made Haiti and was found by a local fisherman. She spends her days helping him catch fish for his family and the local market. I can almost see her now. I imagine her with her mast and rigging gone, torn off by the storm. Nets lay across her deck drying in the hot Caribbean sun, and on the stern the brilliant blue logo, put there with my own hands, *At Ease,* is now stripped away. In its place there are wide course brush stokes in bright red that bear her new name, *Regalo de Dios:* Gift from God.

Bob and Jerry are considering giving the Bermuda race another shot.

The Coast Guardsmen who rescued both the *Almeisan* crew and the *At Ease* crew were fantastic to work with. Because I am not a veteran of the Coast Guard, I had to ask for a great many explanations and help with terminology. Daniel Molthen, Jeremiah Loser, Art "A.J." Thompson, Audie Andry, Donald Eric Bader, and James Geramita all were incredibly patient and giving of their time. I also want to acknowledge flight mechanic Randy Swanz and copilot Andy Barrow, the other two helicopter crewmembers working side by side with Daniel Molthen and Jeremiah Loser on the *At Ease* rescue.

Jeremiah later told me that his mission involving the *At Ease* was good preparation for his involvement in the Hurricane Katrina rescues. "We would sometimes just see waving hands sticking up through holes in the roof of flooded homes. When I would get lowered down from the helicopter there was so much happening at once. People would be screaming at one house, while the next one was on fire, and I had to make lots of quick decisions. The *At Ease* rescue gave me confidence to handle the chaos."

There are dozens of Coast Guard people involved in the *Almeisan* and *At Ease* SAR cases, from ground crews to search and rescue coordinators, whose names did not make it into the book, but without their effort the successful rescues would never have happened. Oftentimes the helicopter crews get all the attention while the C-130 plane crews are not acknowledged. There were no fewer than four C-130s whose crews put in exhausting and dangerous hours flying at low altitudes through the storm, assisting in the *Almeisan* rescue and the search for Loch and Tom. Some of the additional Coast Guard personnel and

AUTHOR'S NOTE AND ACKNOWLEDGMENTS

C-130 crewmembers involved in the rescues are: Karen Anderson, Bruno Baltazar, W. Barrera, Ian Bastek, Matthew Brooks, C. Brown, C. Bublitz, George Cathey, Joseph Deer, Matthew Doscher, Jim Duval, T. Edwards, R. Ferguson, Julie Kuck, D. Levesque, Benjamin Maitre, R. Meacham, J. Mills, Geoffrey Pagels, Libby Pruitt, R. Rademacher, Mark Russell, Wayne Sippola, B. Stough, Bruce Tucker, Brian Wilson, José Zuñiga. To you folks, and to the dozens of other Coasties involved in some way, the survivors and I thank you. That same appreciation also extends to the crew of the *Seay,* the *Trenton,* the *Sakura Express,* the *Castillo de Butrón,* and *Front Brabant.*

The *Almeisan* search and rescue operation was so difficult and unusual it was selected by the Coast Guard as the SAR Case of the Year, a recognition that goes to only one of the thousands of Coast Guard SARs conducted in a twelve-month period.

Ted Weber, captain of the *Cosmos,* were kind enough to answer my questions about his nightmare in the storm, via email from Europe, just before he made a solo crossing of the Atlantic back to the United States. I would never have been aware of the *Cosmos* knockdown if it wasn't for a fine article about the storm and boats in peril written by Douglas Campbell in *Soundings* magazine, and another excellent story written by David Liscio for *Sailing* magazine.

Reviewing early drafts of *Overboard* were my friend and agent Ed Knappman, brother Mark Tougias, and friends Jon Cogswell, Adam Gamble, and Dr. Patrick Kelly. All offered suggestions that were dead-on, and I especially am indebted to Dr. Kelly for helping me with my sailing terminology, pacing of the story, and encouragement when the going got tough. Dr. Kelly read every word of the manuscript and his insights were invaluable. Editor Colin Harrison, assistant editor Jessica Manners, Anne Cherry, Esther Paradelo, and publicists Katherine Monaghan and Meredith Wahl have made this a better book with their suggestions and inspiring words. Sandy Reidy, Laura Ferrer, and Sue Burd were all generous with their time and insights. I also received and appreciated many kind words of support from the people attending my various presentations and speaking engagements. Writing is often a solitary mission and meeting readers in person gives me positive energy.

AUTHOR'S NOTE AND ACKNOWLEDGMENTS

Jon Cogswell and I spent part of a long drive to my cabin in northern Vermont simply trying to nail down the title for the book. Unlike other books I've written, where I knew the title from day one, this story had me torn between four different title alternatives. One of them had *Gulf Stream* in the title because it played such an important role in Loch's survival. And it also may have contributed to the size of the wave that sent Tom hurtling into the sea, snapped the boat's lifeline, and caused Loch to go tumbling out of the raft. Researching the Gulf Stream was fascinating, and it made me think that maybe the so-called Bermuda Triangle mystery—at least for shipping—is nothing more than the Gulf Stream generating waves larger than surrounding waters and sinking boats before they can get out a Mayday.

In the end, after final individual brainstorming sessions with Jon Cogswell, Adam Gamble, and editor Colin Harrison, we decided *Overboard!* was the title to go with: simple, to the point, and in a single word conveys the heart of what happened on the eighth of May, 2005. What a title can never express—but what I hope the book has—is the determination and resiliency displayed by the *Almeisan*'s entire crew in a time of great duress. It was my privilege to write their story.

ABOUT THE AUTHOR

Michael Tougias is a versatile author and coauthor of eighteen books. His best-selling book *Fatal Forecast: An Incredible True Tale of Disaster and Survival at Sea* was praised by the *Los Angeles Times* as "a breathtaking book. . . . [Tougias] spins a marvelous and terrifying yarn." His earlier book, *Ten Hours Until Dawn: The True Story of Heroism and Tragedy Aboard the* Can Do, about a sea rescue during the Blizzard of 1978, was praised by *Booklist* "as the best story of peril at sea since *The Perfect Storm*" and was selected by the American Library Association as an Editor's Choice: One of the Top Books of the Year.

Tougias and coauthor Casey Sherman teamed up and wrote a combination history/ocean rescue story titled *The Finest Hours: The U.S. Coast Guard's Most Daring Sea Rescue.* This drama occurred in 1952 off the coast of Cape Cod when two oil tankers, in the grip of a nor'easter, were split in half and eighty-four lives were in jeopardy.

On a lighter note, Tougias's award-winning humor book *There's a Porcupine in My Outhouse: Misadventures of a Vermont Mountain Man Wannabe* was selected by the Independent Publishers Association as the Best Nature Book of the Year. The author has also written for more than two hundred different and diverse publications, including *The New York Times, Field & Stream, Fine Gardening,* and *The Boston Globe.*

Tougias has prepared slide lectures for all his books, including *Overboard,* and his lecture schedule is posted on his website at www .michaeltougias.com.

Through research into dozens of survival stories, Tougias has also prepared an inspirational lecture for businesses and organizations titled *Survival Lessons: Peak Performance & Decision-Making Under*

Pressure. Tougias describes this presentation as "an uplifting way to learn some practical strategies and mind-sets for achieving difficult goals from those who have survived against all odds." He has given the presentation for all types of organizations, including General Dynamics, the Massachusetts School Library Association, NYU Surgeons' Roundtable, Lincoln Financial Services, Goodwin Proctor Law Firm, and many more. Interested organizations can contact him at michaeltougias@yahoo.com or P.O. Box 72, Norfolk, MA 02056.

SUMMARY OF MICHAEL J. TOUGIAS'S LATEST BOOKS

The Finest Hours: The True Story of the
U.S. Coast Guard's Most Daring Sea Rescue
(Coauthored with Casey Sherman)

On February 18, 1952, an astonishing maritime event began when a ferocious nor'easter split in half a five-hundred-foot-long oil tanker, the *Pendleton,* approximately one mile off the coast of Cape Cod, Massachusetts. Incredibly, just twenty miles away, a second oil tanker, the *Fort Mercer,* also split in half. On both fractured tankers, men were trapped on the severed bows and sterns, and all four sections were sinking in sixty-foot seas. Thus began a life-and-death drama of survival, heroism, and tragedy. Of the eighty-four seamen aboard the tankers, seventy would be rescued and fourteen would lose their lives.

Going to the rescue of the *Pendleton*'s stern section were four young Coast Guardsmen in a thirty-six-foot lifeboat—a potential suicide mission in such a small vessel. Standing between the men and their mission were towering waves that reached seventy feet, blinding snow, and one of the most dangerous shoals in the world, the dreaded Chatham Bar. The waters along the outer arm of Cape Cod are called the graveyard of the Atlantic for good reason, yet this rescue defied all odds when thirty-two survivors were crammed into the tiny lifeboat and brought to safety (Coast Guard officials later said that "the rescue is unparalleled in the entire annals of maritime history").

Several cutters and small boats raced to the sinking sections of the *Fort Mercer,* and valiant rescue attempts were undertaken: some successful, some not.

"A blockbuster account of tragedy at sea . . . gives a you-are-there feel."

—*The Providence Journal*

"A gripping read!"

—James Bradley, author of *Flags of Our Fathers*

Fatal Forecast: An Incredible True Tale of
Disaster and Survival at Sea

On a cold November day in 1980, two fishing vessels, the *Fair Wind* and the *Sea Fever,* set out from Cape Cod to catch offshore lobsters at Georges Bank. The National Weather Service had forecast typical fall weather in the area for the next three days—even though the organization knew that its only weather buoy at Georges Bank was malfunctioning. Soon after the boats reached the fishing ground, they were hit with hurricane-force winds and massive, sixty-foot waves that battered the boats for hours. The captains and crews struggled heroically to keep their vessels afloat in the unrelenting storm. One monstrous wave of ninety- to one-hundred feet soon capsized the *Fair Wind,* trapping the crew inside. Meanwhile, on the *Sea Fever,* Captain Peter Brown (whose father owned the *Andrea Gail* of *The Perfect Storm* fame) did his best to ride out the storm, but a giant wave blew out one side of the pilothouse, sending a crewmember into the churning ocean.

Meticulously researched and vividly told, *Fatal Forecast* is first and foremost a tale of miraculous survival. Most amazing is the story of Ernie Hazard, who had managed to crawl inside a tiny inflatable life raft—only to be repeatedly thrown into the ocean as he fought to endure more than fifty hours adrift in the storm-tossed seas. By turns tragic, thrilling, and inspiring, Ernie's story deserves a place among the greatest survival tales ever told.

As gripping and harrowing as *The Perfect Storm*—but with a miracle ending—*Fatal Forecast* is an unforgettable true story about the collision of two spectacular forces: the brutality of nature and the human will to survive.

> "Tougias skillfully submerges us in this storm and spins a marvelous and terrifying yarn. He makes us fight alongside Ernie Hazard and cheer as he is saved . . . a breathtaking book."
>
> —*Los Angeles Times*
>
> "Ernie Hazard's experiences, as related by Tougias, deserve a place as a classic of sea survival history."
>
> —*The Boston Globe*
>
> "Tougias spins a dramatic saga. . . . (He) has written eighteen books and this is among his most gripping."
>
> —*National Geographic Adventure Magazine*